EDUCATION: Planning and Human Development

EDUCATION

Planning and Human Development

(In 8 Volumes)

Technology and Development of Distance Education

(Volume 4)

V.C. PANDEY

ISHA BOOKS

DELHI—110 033

EDUCATION: Planning and Human Development
(Education)

Rs. 7000 (Set in 8 Vols.)

ISBN: 81-8205-006-5 (Set)
ISBN: 81-8205-010-3 (Vol. 4)

Published in 2003 in India by
Isha Books, D-43, Prithviraj Road
Adarsh Nagar, Delhi-110 033

Lasertypesetting by: Varsha Graphics, Delhi
Printed at: Chawla Offset Press, Delhi

Preface

Within a context of rapid technological change and shifting market conditions, the education system is challenged with providing increased educational opportunities without increased budgets. Many educational institutions are answering this challenge by developing distance education programs. At its most basic level, distance education takes place when a teacher and student(s) are separated by physical distance, and technology, often in concert with face-to-face communication, is used to bridge the instructional gap. These types of programs can provide adults with a second chance at a college education, reach those disadvantaged by limited time, distance or physical disability, and update the knowledge base of workers at their places of employment.

In recent years, educators have witnessed the rapid development of computer networks, dramatic improvements in the processing power of personal computers, and striking advances in magnetic storage technology. These developments have made the computer a dynamic force in distance education, providing a new and interactive means of overcoming time and distance to reach learners. Distance educators can use the internet and world wide web to help students gain a basic understanding of how to navigate and take full advantage of the networked world into which they will be graduating.

Although technology plays a key role in the delivery of distance education, educators must remain focused on instructional outcomes, not the technology of delivery. The key to effective distance education is focusing on the needs of the learners, the requirements of the content, and the constraints faced by the teacher, before selecting a delivery system.

This book presents the ways in which technology can enhance distance learning and calls on educators to take a leadership role in determining the ways in which technology is used to support educational goals.

Editor

Contents

1

Distance Education in Infoage

Education systems are today in a position to take up the challenge of the new information and communication technologies. The present information environment is characterized by the mass advent of digital solutions which are drastically changing established realities. Universities, particularly those in the most developed countries, have contributed tremendously in terms of research to the emergence of the new information technologies.

Since the invention of the Internet Protocol (IP) by Vincent Cerf in 1974, it has taken only 15 years to create the basis of collective intelligence. However, universities have been concentrating their efforts mainly on researching and prototyping new tools and have not been attending to the socialization of those tools. Little attention has been devoted to studying their uses.

It is the education and training field, one of the essential activities of modern society, which has benefited least from the contribution of the new information and communication technologies. And it is also this sector which, depending on the direction taken by the changes imposed by globalization and international competition, will either benefit or suffer from developments in terms of content, methods and resources.

The role played by education software in distance education increased in the period from 1985 to 1995 as it gradually replaced learner-controlled approach instruction or programmed education, in which traditional or audiovisual teaching aids were used. By the year 2000, this development process will have been transformed and broadened, relocating learners and teachers, reconstructing the underpinnings of natural course progression, channelling reliable and enriched material through the data transmission networks, combining the necessary documentation with lectures, and enabling teachers, researchers and students to exchange information via electronic mail and forums and thus globalizing knowledge.

The current information context is characterized by the mass advent of digital solutions, which are drastically changing established realities, and by a major risk of the hegemony of one single language to the detriment of multilingualism and of one single culture to the detriment of plurality, in particular through the very rapid development of the Internet, by the atomized development of the new technologies at different paces in different countries and regions and, finally, by the reduced visibility of non-digitized material for ever-growing communities. In parallel, needs are steadily expanding in terms of information and of methods and tools for producing, organizing, disseminating and consulting it.

Most of the technical and methodological solutions necessary to this circulation of information, such as the Internet and related standards, have their origin in the scientific community, which must now devote thought to its uses and its inescapable penetration of the world of education and research. Past experience will have to be analysed in the light of the impact of the digital, particularly on the circulation and transmission of knowledge.

The ICT are revolutionizing the educational fields and enabling them to emerge from arcane debate and the scepticism of educationists, and become a global industry. Whereas the question of the didactic quality of distance education is still the subject of much debate dividing 'traditionalists' and 'specialists', the NICT are beginning to introduce all the factors of what amounts to an educational revolution, in which the teacher-learner and the learner-learner relationship will change radically.

The concepts of 'collaboration' and 'asynchronous education' should gradually become established, more because they reflect the necessities of the evolution of society than for purely educational reasons. This change contains a veritable educational revolution in embryo, in which the traditionally rigid space-time-hierarchy structures will be shattered.

The main argument in favour of this change is, of course, economic; but it must be borne in mind that distance education fees are still as high as those charged for traditional education, since the mass economies that will offset an initial outlay higher, in every respect, than that involved in traditional education, have not yet been achieved. This will change radically as the mass application of this technology becomes established -

which could be the case after a transition period of several years.

There are, of course, still many challenges to be faced: the use of various technologies in appropriate proportions and applications, the question of the evaluation of learners and teachers, the question of intellectual property where educational material is concerned, and the major bottleneck: training in the skilled use of these new tools. The large number of different terms and expressions used in the context of distance or virtual education warrants semantic examination so that they can be classified, misunderstandings can be avoided and the major past and future trends highlighted.

— *Correspondence courses*: characteristic of the first applications which merely used the postal services to overcome distances.

— *Distance education*: used mainly by education experts, existed before the rapid development of the NICT, and seems to be resisting technological change. The term might suffer from the fact that a number of education experts are lagging behind in the technological field, but it should retain its status as a term of reference Distance teaching/distance learning/distance-teaching university: characteristic of the audiovisual (televised) stage of distance education and facing a serious threat from the novel contribution of the NICT.

— *The open university*: places emphasis on the collaborative and global aspects. The collaborative or co-operative university: places emphasis on the aspect of collaboration, both between teachers and learners and between education partners.

— *Asynchronous education*: places emphasis on one of the fundamental aspects of the new style in education which technology has made possible, i.e. studying at one's own pace with no constraints as regards time.

— *The global university*: places emphasis on the geopolitical vision. Computer-mediated education and distributive learning are used by technology specialists.

— *The Internet university*: technological and commercial. Often a 'meta-university' which sells logistic apparatus (software and the Web) with which the purchaser can produce educational material intended for distance distribution.

— *The virtual university*: characteristic of the advanced technology approach (Internet). Sees itself as an integrative concept of the new paradigm, in which physical space and the need for synchrony disappear. One could add a semantic restriction towards higher education, however, whereas in the new paradigm the education field tends to reduce the boundaries between the various types of studies . The virtual campus is a variation of the above, perhaps less open. The concept of the virtual university is the most widespread at the present time.

Concept of the virtual university

Virtual universities use NICT and a combination of the various technological tools 'in proportion' with a view to radically changing the equation of the cost of education. Teaching accompanies the new technological paradigm makes possible:

— asynchronous learning;

— a new inter-actor relationship;

— continuing education;

— a participatory vision of education;

In virtual university there are three areas intersect:

— the area of possibility;

— the technology area;

— the teaching area.

In the area of possibility we can distinguish between an economic revolution democratizing education and the tendency for the compartmentalization of the various forms of education (primary, secondary, university, adult, vocational, and continuing) to disappear.

In the technology area, the NICT are at the top of the hierarchy, but it must be realized that unless these technologies are applied with the appropriate teaching methods, they will add nothing to education but confusion and mistaken objectives.

If, on the other hand, they are mastered, the change of paradigm which they will bring will allow of nothing short of a revolution in teaching, marked primarily by the abandonment of the vertical form of education (vertical transfer of knowledge) in favour of a ring structure, in which the teacher becomes the facilitator of a process which is focused on the learner and on his or her ability to discover knowledge at his or her own pace and in collaboration with other learners and facilitators.

Secondly, as the result of an asynchronous mode of operation, this new form of teaching will ease the constraints of space and time. By losing its verticality, learning becomes a process of collaboration and partnership among various groups. The teaching area is undergoing far-reaching changes. Some recent inputs have been disqualified to a certain extent by technological change, and concepts are currently being revised from the point of view of means and objectives.

The major challenge is to devise a new form of teaching which is based on and transcends technological devices without adopting the attitude of a technologist or mythifying technology. The challenge appears to be less contradictory whenever the sociological aspects accompanying the technological revolution are emphasized.

After several years of slow and difficult progress, this discipline has entered a 'push technology' phase, which could come to maturity in less than two years and could give way to a new global market-driven phase, in which market shares will grow significantly in less than five years.

We are in a situation similar to that of the Internet in 1992; we are going through a two- to three-year period of transition, which will be followed by a period of tremendous expansion. The following are the three key factors in the 'push technology':

1. the necessary change in teaching methods, and in the student-teacher and student-student relationship in particular;
2. the key ingredients for the change in teaching methods: the pursuit of group interactiveness and proactiveness (collaboration);
3. determination of the judicious proportion of technological facilities.

On the bases thus obtained, the market will then begin to direct options along several lines, which will not necessarily be coherent: emergence of global and distance academic proposals in the main languages (English, Spanish, French, followed by the oriental and Asian languages) competing on the global education market, and the gradual and appreciable reduction of costs as a result of mass development; emergence of a global run-of-the-mill education 'bazaar', in which purely mercenary aims and the question of intellectual property will become crucial unless the development of the Internet in the next five years begins to give clues to solutions.

Virtual university projects

No project has as yet proved supreme in all aspects of the virtual university. Some projects have attained a very high level in some of these aspects, but generally show deficiencies in other essential parameters of NICT-based distance education. The most promising projects are those which are based on an infrastructure and a historical development and which have succeeded in keeping abreast of technological advances (the Open University in the United Kingdom, Canadian projects, etc.).

A distinction must first be made between virtual university projects and projects which are intended to serve such projects. The latter, which we term 'meta-projects' are to be found in several different areas: the creation of (telecom and/or software) infrastructures, such as Internet 2, projects of major manufacturers or commercial projects; the creation of transportable material; the creation of co-operation structures.

The US Science Foundation, which supported the Internet international telecommunications skeleton for many years, suspended its efforts in 1993 to give way to the commercial Internet. After three years of discussion of the importance of allowing the market to take over advanced development, Internet 2 marks the return of the university initiative and, ultimately, it is a question of organizing the transmission band in order to make distance education possible.

The Europeans have projects which are similar - DANTE in particular - but which are perhaps less geared to building up the infrastructure for distance education. *Worldspace* This network of geostationary satellites for digital radio is under construction. As of 1999, it will cover all countries with emergent economies, that is to say, a total of over 4 billion people; 10 per cent of the channels will be devoted to education and training, a fact which will make it the most powerful educational instrument in the service of developing countries.

The persons responsible for higher education in the countries concerned will be invited to take part in the measures to define and establish appropriate programmes, to assist in the development of appropriate methodologies suited to this new digital technology, and to turn it to good account in all of their fields of competence, particularly that of teacher training.

In Latin America A number of experiments are being carried out in Latin America. They can be divided into four main categories:

(a) several national or regional projects, which are primarily instructional in orientation but which are having great difficulty in keeping abreast of and applying technological advancement (UNA, CREAD, etc.);

(b) projects involving considerable investment in technology and a notable strategic capacity for regional establishment, offset by relative weakness regarding the research, sociocultural vision and regional integration complex (UV/ITESM, Chilean projects);

(c) several initiatives (in Argentina in particular) which have a notable socio-political vision but which lack the means of having any noteworthy regional impact (Lund, Fasta, Cediproae, etc.) and remain one-off initiatives;

(d) the Monterey virtual university project (Mexico), which, despite several shortcomings regarding sociocultural and geopolitical aspects, shows that advances in the field of initial outlay and technological control may prove essential in the regionalization/internationalization of education markets.

The World Bank project for Africa (AVU) is a series of courses of instruction in scientific disciplines offered in the form of university bachelor's and master's degree courses and continuing education units, and is common to many countries. It is placed at the disposal of African countries against payment of a fee. The project uses the NICT, particularly satellite broadcasting from the United States via INTELSAT 515. The courses are divided into three sub-series - English language, Portuguese language and French language. The World Bank has initially appealed to France, Belgium and Switzerland in the case of the French-language section, and a pilot experiment is under way.

The first is the Institute for Information Technology n Education, which was set up in Moscow by UNESCO and the Government of the Russian Federation in February 1997 at the conclusion of the International Congress on Education and Informatics. Its main objective is very ambitious - that of elaborating a model of global continuing education for all.

Another project naned as Swis aims to promote the conveyance of information to society. The FU.NT group proposes to create a Swiss virtual campus. According to this concept, institutes of higher education should, on the one hand, be encouraged to redesign some of their courses to make them accessible in electronic form and, on the other, they should be invited to allow their own students to obtain credits through the network by taking courses whose quality will have to be guaranteed by an accreditation process.' By 2000-2003, it should be possible to achieve important objectives through joint action by institutes of higher education at Confederation and Canton level, such as action to improve the quality of the educational experience for students, to transform university teaching and to provide new opportunities of access to higher education, to reduce costs - at least per student, and to provide a better supply of further education.

In North America Penn State University: the American historical reference The virtual campus of Stanford University Simon Fraser University, British Columbia, one of the major Canadian projects A national university education network is being built up in Canada, which, it is planned, will operate via the Internet and interactive videoconferencing, thus linking the 12 Canadian establishments and gathering all of their programmes together with a view to providing young French speakers with as wide a range of studies in French as possible. The driving force behind this project is the University of Ottawa; this showcase of official bilingualism is situated in the province of Ontario, the home of half of the French speakers outside Quebec, and offers a very rich palette of programmes. Furthermore, the University has been running a distance education network extending throughout the province for the past five years. The UFHQ of Eastern Canada, which are fairly well equipped, have also already offered and received distance courses.

The AUPELF-UREF French-language project is a sort of 'French-language virtual meta-university', which, depending on the means available and the strategic options defined, could provide a backup for existing French-language universities in terms of: distance education infrastructure placed at their disposal; advice and assistance in the creation of the necessary structures; shared educational material; technical means and human resources for facilitating the preparation of on-line educational material.

Changes in Education

The paradigm shift in education is evolving through three successive models. they are:

Model	*Focus*	*Role of the student*	*Technology*
traditional	teacher	passive	blackboard/TV/radio
information	student	active	PC
knowledge	group	adaptive	PC + network

The conditions are now ripe for a model based on knowledge. Technologies (mainly the NICT) are playing a key role in this paradigm shift. The key factors in the paradigm shift are as follows:

Factor	Development
Time	The time factor will no longer be a constraint. Asynchronous education frees the student from the demands of time.
Space	The distance factor will no longer be a constraint. The student can take part in education without needing to be present in person at the university.
Cost	The pedagogical investment for modern distance education is certainly greater than that of the traditional model, whether in terms of initial outlay or the investment connected with delivering the education. There are two factors, however, which will reduce the overall cost in factors of scale: 1. the reduction of needs in terms of area and premises; 2. the appreciable increase in the size of the virtual class.
Relationships	The traditionally vertical teacher-student relationship will evolve towards a more horizontal model, in which the teacher becomes a facilitator, expert or colleague and the learner becomes naturally active. In this evolution of roles the group will gain importance as a place for consultation, dialogue and collaboration. Through this mechanism the education is 'received' by the individual in interaction with a group, of which the teachers constitute only one element. Roles are thus completely redefined, and the dynamism of the new roles requires a new student.
Information/ knowledge	The transfer of knowledge is no longer the primary object of education. The student must learn to acquire information as the need arises, to evaluate it, and to transform it into knowledge through the relational process.

Market	By easing the constraints of space and time, education will open up to the global market, where language will become one of the main constraints on expansion.
Competition/ Collaboration	The internationalization of the education market and the emergence of new entities placed deliberately in the commercial area will intensify competition between educational establishments. In parallel, collaboration and strategic alliances on the part of universities will become imperative as the appropriate response to change.
Assessment	The traditional concepts of student assessment based on (examination) results will have to be adapted to new methods in which the assessment of the process will gain more importance so that the measuring of assimilated knowledge can be circumvented and factors more sensitive to the equation of the new professional can be integrated: ability to carry out research, to adapt, to communicate, to collaborate, etc.
Type	The distinctions drawn between the various types of education (primary, secondary, technical, university, vocational) will become less important, and the emphasis will be placed on continuing education.

The advent of the NICT in the years that lie ahead raises the question of how the teaching profession can prepare for these radical changes. Structurally, distance education is much more demanding as regards teaching ability. The 'new teachers' will have to *master* this new NICT environment and be *mentally* prepared for a radical change of role while adding to and *updating* their knowledge of their special subjects.

Appropriate training in the NICT, providing an integral vision of the discipline with emphasis on the 'information culture', is a key factor in the successful preparation of teachers. It will provide a means of accompanying the psychological aspect and of reassuring teachers as regards keeping abreast of developments.

The new teachers will emerge from the isolation of the classroom and receive considerable logistical support, and it is up to them to be able to co-ordinate and use it: they must have production specialists at their disposal for both audiovisual means and the Web, so that they can achieve high-quality results as regards form and can *concentrate on content*, i.e. on the educational material. The realization by university authorities of the need to provide teachers with a set of support functions is a key factor in successful educational production.

As regards the optimal course of procedure of the virtual class and the emergence of the group learning process - the group constituting the creative centre in the new set-up - the management of the virtual community linking teachers and students is the crucial factor.

The utmost attention must be devoted to the methods, procedures and software underlying group communication. Over and above any other logistical element, this factor is the key to the successful dynamic of the virtual class, whereas it is one of .the lesser investments. The production of interactive multimedia as personal learning tools complementing network-based tools seems to be reserved for industry for the time being, and distance universities are slow to apply themselves to this field.

Web-based educational sites are to be observed which have excellent graphic models but response speeds which are too low to serve as an educational tool - a fact which argues in favour of producing interactive CD-ROMs and implementing intranets rapidly. Moreover, the emergence of digital radio (DAB) has made it possible to found new hopes on the mass dissemination of knowledge at low cost and in acceptable conditions.

This technology is particularly suited to developing countries. UNESCO recommends that 'design templates' be created for educational software. Thus, the suppliers of course material will be able to offer programmes in the language of their choice, regardless of the region of the world. Each producer will be supplied with a compendium of examples of good practice in using NICT-related software. This action should enable the countries of the South to develop good-quality open and distance education rapidly.

Virtual Reference Libraries

Information is becoming globalized; it is becoming an inescapable market framed by strict laws. The need is growing for measures to defend freedom of access to information in the form of a universal public service intended for the research and education sector in particular. Considerable efforts to put informal literature, reports and theses on line are becoming a matter of priority.

The same applies to free software designed according to the ideas of the producer groups; the LINUX operating system and the CDS-ISIS documentary software can be quoted as examples. Multilingualism is an important point in the defence of cultural pluralism as opposed to the monolingualism of information.

Automatic translation tools must be implemented rapidly. The purpose of virtual reference libraries and electronic libraries is to provide all scientists, researchers, teachers, and students with a virtual information site through which they can access all the products necessary to their education, training and research work.

The concept is based on the provision of a series of services which are not conditioned by distance or time. Various types of product can be provided:

— *Databases and directories*: Directories of teachers and researchers and directories of establishments and training courses are supplemented by specialized databases, indexes of theses and grey literature, and all of the databases available in the French-speaking world. These databases cover all fields of science, the economy, technology and the press.

— *Knowledge bases*: Numerous knowledge bases have been structured and are available, but they are scattered throughout the world. They must be identified and located so that they can be made available to the scientific world.

— *Selective data diffusion (SDD)*: Students who have prepared dissertations can benefit from the SDD programme, through which, once the user's need has been analysed, every user can be provided with a profile for the diffusion of updated or retrospective data pertaining to his or her research.

— *Full texts of books and journals*: A number of scientific books and journals have been or are in the process of being digitized. They must be made available to universities free of charge.

— *Research notes, lecture notes and technical data sheets*: There are many documents of this nature in the informal literature. They are necessary for updating knowledge and development, yet they are often unexploited. Once validated, the compilation of these documents should provide a means of circulating research work more usefully.

— *Theses and dissertations*: The aim is to make known and disseminate the tremendous amount of knowledge contained in these documents, which are rarely published. Researchers will thus be able to find partially-produced theses in databanks and then obtain the documents in full or in part. A global digitization site must be launched without delay. It will be possible for the collection of written documents to be tele-edited. Tele-editing is a means of disseminating a document on request without incurring printing and delivery costs.

— *Software and interfaces*: There is a plethora of software, freeware or shareware, often created by universities and available on the networks according to the acquisition rules specific to this type of tool. An inventory will have to be drawn up to begin with and the scientific products will have to be analysed.

— *Educational software*: This software has several functions: a learning-aid function, a simulation function and an evaluation function.

Trraining Programmes

The human factor is one of the major factors curbing NICT penetration of higher education. Before any technological action can be taken, training programmes need to be defined at various levels for various target groups.

Plans must be made for training technicians and engineers to back up technology within institutes of education and research, for training teachers, and for training decision-makers. The latter is a *sine qua non* if the NICT are to enter the scientific world. It is essential to convince the political and institutional authorities that these technologies are justified as a factor of development and modernity. One approach to development is to train instructors in the NICT by using the NICT.

Three objectives can be envisaged through the training of specialists:

- — demonstrating NICT potential and promoting the appropriation of these technologies in the regions;
- — achieving the critical mass of technical specialists in a given sector for a given region;
- — increasing teacher potential by contributing a methodology and education tools which can be re-used by trainees who are later called upon to become trainers themselves.

The countries of the North have long established national policies for training teachers in the NICT, but this is not always the case in the countries of the South, which are liable to lag farther and farther behind - a factor which will exacerbate the imbalance between North and South. Sustainable action Training workshops must meet the expectations of the academic world in order to help it to master the NICT. To do so they must go beyond the strictly technical context as part of a more comprehensive plan for sustainable development. In these training courses just as much importance must be attached to content as to form and the role and mission of the trainers must be explained so as to create a real climate of technical and cultural co-operation. The courses must be based on lectures and case studies and take the form of training/action.

Implementation of Distance Learning Programmes

Before we address the critical factors to successfully implement technology in instruction we must be prepared to answer the question of why this is important. In most cases this question will come from current educational dministrators/faculty, governmental bodies, or other funding agencies. Why do we need to use this expensive equipment and technology to teach? For those of us who have seen the awesome possibilities of educational technology the answer is clear:

— To improve access

— To reduce cost/increase efficiency

— To improve quality

— To provide "on demand " or "just in time " learning

— To allow a learner centred approach in an asynchronous or real time model

There are innumerable examples in the research literature that discuss the five factors listed above and their importance to successful educational technology programmes. There is no question that the use of technology can improve access to education for those bound by geographic remoteness, physical handicap, or jobs that preclude them from being physically present at a traditional university. The expense of developing and presenting courses for small numbers of students is often a problem in small states.

The rapid changes precipitated by technology and market demands on the educational enterprise will require nothing less than a major shift in the ways colleges and universities do business. It is somewhat disconcerting that many institutions believe that they can survive by avoiding these changes. Many are paralyzed by the insanity principle of continuing to do things the same way and yet expecting different outcomes. Institutions that define university outreach in concert with a self-serving parochialism will find themselves out of business.

As those of us in small states look at providing quality educational programmes to dispersed audiences on a small budget we must make our funding sources, public or private, aware of the advantages of this method of instruction. Only after we have satisfied ourselves and others that electronically mediated learning is a valid and worthwhile concept will we be able to look at the critical factors required to successfully implement technology in instruction.

The most critical factors to successfully implement technology in instruction are:

— A need for the programme

— Institutional "buy in " and support from administration and faculty.

— Quality instructional content

— Student support services

— Technology resources

Most of these factors are self-explanatory but a few words about student support services might be helpful. In order for the distance learning programme to be successful the institution must provide the remote student the same level of support as the on-campus student or, in some areas, more. For example, electronic office hours by the professor (for example by e-mail or interactive video), course registration, materials distribution and delivery, access to the library on-line, and training to use the technology are critical to the success of any programme. There may be many other areas of student support each institution must address but the critical factor is that the remote student should not be penalized for being at a distance.

The critical factors, in rank order, required to successfully implement technology in instruction are as follows:

— Identified need for the programme

— Faculty supportive and given incentives for motivation

— Funds for capital costs:production, equipment, facilities

— Availability of on-going money for operations and expenses

— Quality of educational content of the programme

— Adequate support staff to produce the programme

— Ensuring equivalent learning experience to remote students

— Enthusiasm and belief by the institution in the overall distance learning project

— Identification of a visible, spirited key leader/ administrator initiating the programme
— Adequate receive sites, facilities, and staff
— Availability of appropriate and specialized equipment to deliver the courses
— Sufficient time for careful needs analysis of the student population
— Ensuring equivalent status for remote students:i. e. credit, degree
— Support for quality instructional design
— Identification of a marketing plan for the courses

Professional Development

Continuing professional development may even be a determining influence on levels of economic development when lifelong study, as well as training and re-training, are possible and taken for granted by large fractions of the population. This readiness to learn greatly increases the capacity of a labour force to respond to rapid technological change and is at least as important as the innovations that support it, or the competitive markets that drive it. Since learning in the knowledge society can no longer be narrowly equated with the transfer of specific established content, the very nature of professional education is shifting.

Modern mass higher education teaches people not to become too closely devoted to one occupation or a single set of skills. It prepares them for the likelihood that both will change often and that they must travel fast. To travel fast one must travel light, in skills as well as attitudes.

The only skill that does not become obsolete is the skill of learning new skills. The learning trajectories of professionals will become increasingly contextualized and individual. At the same time, the challenge of globalization to the maintenance of local values and identity in education is increasing. No country can afford to disregard education for participation in the knowledge economy. The knowledge economy offers exponential returns on investment in education. Investment in education will now have to be geared towards the knowledge economy. This concerns all developing countries, whatever their performance over the past decade in the field of basic education.

If we lose the connecting links between basic education for all and the high-powered knowledge economy, we risk opening up a vast chasm separating poor and rich countries. A paradoxical consequence is that, despite the potential for information and communication technologies (ICTs) to provide "opportunities to build local knowledge structures, which can in turn be shared with a larger audience in the context of our global society ", existing educational systems straining to meet greater demand may be driven to accepting ready-made technology-based solutions.

Educators believe that the failures of many past educational technology applications have been due to the fact that they were ill-adapted to the culture of the learners, insufficiently interactive, too expensive or tried to replace rather than re-inforce the role of the teacher.

From the organizational perspective, there are evident advantages of deploying ICTs in continuing professional development at a distance. For provider institutions targeting specialized and scattered groups, communication technologies facilitate gathering a critical mass of learners, and monitoring the progress of distributed learner populations.

For course organizers, information in digital formats offers just-in-time resources, rapid transfer and ready accessibility of learning and research resources.

For students and tutors at any individual location, ICT-based delivery increases the range of opportunities for acquiring new skills and for professional updating, and can also create a base for professional networking and peer support.

A recent survey of the costs of networked learning in the UK identified unattributed staff time, and time and resource demands on students (including acquisition of hardware, printing of learning materials) as significant elements. Thus there may be divergence, or even tension, between institutional, staff and student interests in the deployment of ICTs. By way of example, the e- mail list model, a course support mechanism with very low entry costs, building on well-established working practices and software environments, does over the longer term tend to foster a centre- periphery pattern of communication which can overload tutor time and also carries the risk of encouraging dependence rather than self-direction among students.

When we come to consider the impact of the new technologies on quality of learning, questions proliferate. A recent meta-analysis by Hara and Kling confirms a current of thinking among online learning practitioners that there is a gap between the appreciation of the course delivery potential represented by ICTs, and the understanding of what makes for effective transferable learning and positive experiences for staff and students.

For the andragogical approach, which sees students as a major resource for each other 's learning development, this is a crucial issue. Social learning has been poorly served by traditional distance learning methods.

The constraint imposed on contingent dialogue between tutors and students and amongst students themselves in distance learning inevitably imposes limitations on social constructivist activities. From this perspective, the key advantage of ICTs is their potential for increasing the opportunities for mutual exchange, or for interaction through simulated co-presence. Indeed this is often a major objective in bringing a professional development course online.

Realizing the apparent andragogical opportunities, particularly in the area of overcoming the tutor-centred model of teaching and learning, and enhancing learning dialogue among students, is not straightforward. Nor should we be surprised if professional development students online sometimes show less of the mature learner characteristic of self-directedness than might have been anticipated from their knowledge, experience, and general learning skills. Given that the autonomy of adult learners is context-dependent, computer- supported group communication is in itself a sufficiently new context to pose challenges additional to those of new domain knowledge.

Emerging in parallel with the "hidden costs literature referred to above is an "effectiveness of learning " literature from researchers who have been involved in pedagogical experiments with ICTs, or close to them in evaluation of outcomes, a literature that asks questions about existing examples or about best deployment of communication resources in support of learning from online dialogue.

For small professional development groups, there are three quite different sources of difficulty: pragmatically, technical problems;in relation to the learning design, ambiguity or uncertainty;and in interaction, the need for swifter and more detailed feedback. While all of these are significant, the first writer 's own investigations in the recorded online interactions of adult learners suggest that none of these sources of difficulty can be entirely isolated from issues around expectation and prior experience – with even the overtly technical sometimes representing a displacement of other kinds of concern.

Despite a long-standing acceptance of the liberating effects of computer-mediated communications on reticent individuals some recent empirical work has suggested there may be critical thresholds for confident and effective engagement which some online course members may never attain, and there is some support for this from the students. A sense of social connectedness appears to be a contributing factor or perhaps even a prerequisite for learning through participation in a discursive environment.

Detailed comparison of working groups further suggests that communicative patterns may be significantly group-contextual and that their development through trial and error is liable to absorb considerable time and energy. Issues of structuring the learning experience have also emerged:too many channels in the software environment may inhibit learning; while structured induction into discussion activities is vital, even after the initial steep learning curve the management of uncertainty and isolation in the online environment remains a problem for a substantial proportion of students, and so scaffolding devices have a continuing role.

The genuinely dialectic learning exchange central to the social constructivist model is not common from online interaction, though their experiments also suggest that such skills can be acquired, and that modelling in the course context through structured exercises and examples contributes to their acquisition.

Individual reflective learning could easily remain invisible, and can be undervalued:"Silence is seen as non-participation when in fact it could simply be that someone is trying to think about what is happening and perhaps trying to make connections with either their practice or the debate or indeed the readings ". This produces a fundamental problem for assessing learning from the online evidence alone – for example, , in grading students for their online participation. But at the same time it points towards ways of working with students to engage with the changing purposes and needs they bring to the online situation, or acknowledging that online discussion may be the occasion, rather than the site, of a developing understanding, and setting the scope of online activity accordingly. Through activities such as scheduled reflective discussions or personal journal keeping, or by addressing needs arising from the offline professional situation through mutual support groups or information exchanges, the resources of the online environment can be deployed to build bridges with students ' wider experiences of learning.

While course-related induction and ongoing support are crucial to effective development of online discussion, the support of an integrated course design is also indispensable;and that alternative forms of discursive software environments should to be taken into account, and related to the broader learning aims for the course.

Overall, five-phase schema of motivation, socialization, information exchange, knowledge construction and development can offer a strong generic framework for courses introducing adult learners to a discursive online environment, although its application to different learning situations remains to be investigated.

Learners participate differentially in structured online activities, with individuals favouring those modes to which they relate most readily – which are likely to be influenced by factors such as domain experience or personal background.

Challenges

Various factors must be taken into account when the NICT are being introduced into higher education - an undertaking which is not without risks. The economic imbalance between the countries of the North and those of the South disqualifies the latter. There are several factors which determine this imbalance:

— universities do not all have flat-rate connection;

— it is paradoxical that the poorest countries should be those where the cost of telecommunications is highest;

— computers are still expensive and heavily taxed in those countries, although the states are beginning to pursue incentive policies;

— universities are undergoing a reorganization whose contours are still vague and not yet fully understood;

— there is a risk of cultural uniformization unless diversity - linguistic diversity in particular - is assured;

— there is a gap between the academic world and the industrial world;

— there is a risk of de-skilling in the case of teachers who cannot or do not want to adapt to the new circumstances;

— de facto technological imperialism entails the risk of cultural imperialism if only one part of the world produces material and the other consumes it.

When one acknowledges that the mass advent of the new information and communication technologies in all activities in our societies is an inescapable fact, it becomes vital for the education and training field to benefit rapidly and as a priority from what these NICT have brought. These technologies will revolutionize teaching on an economic, cultural and social basis. Furthermore, since training is becoming a market in the context of globalization, the following aspects must be taken into account when broaching the problem: the fact that the NICT must be used and the various technological tools combined 'in proportion' with a view to a radical change in the equation of the cost of education; the educational methods which will accompany the new technological paradigm and which will lead to:

— asynchronous learning;

— a new inter-actor relationship;

— 'lifelong' education;

— a participatory vision of the educational act.

The following aspects will have to be incorporated into the new forms of transmission of knowledge in the near future:

— regional diversity;

— co-development;

— scientific excellence;

— intellectual property;

— portability of teaching material;

— the quality approach.

As a mediator of knowledge, the new teachers must thus be placed in an effective logistic environment so that they can concentrate on the expertise of learning the scientific content of their discipline. This idea must be taken fully on board by those in charge in the academic world if the production of education is to be successful. The management of the virtual community must be based on strong logistics regarding methods, procedures and software, which will facilitate the transmission of knowledge as well as the inter-actor relationship.

Decision-makers must be sensitized without delay and the actors must be trained in the use of these new technologies and in their uses for transmitting knowledge. The 'template' software tools must also be defined jointly and must be free and easy for the scientific academic community to appropriate; thought must furthermore be devoted to defining research projects in connection with this new field of problems.

2

Use of ICTs in Distance Education

The post-modern world is decentered, constantly changing, without the chains and conventions of modern society. The liberative potentials unleashed by this global movement of pragmatism started manifesting themselves in the new global order during the 1960s and 1970s - the student movement, environment movement, the Information age, the new consumerism, the multinational capital, women's movement etc. This time round, all the disciplines including education working hitherto under a unifying theoretical framework of "modernization" came under assaults from several quarters.

Distance and open education (DOE) represents a paradigm shift in the world of education. Emergence of distance and open education can be traced to the decline of an education system besieged by anti-modernization assaults. As an important sector, there is more to DOE than a substantial sharing of post-modernist facilities of the new information technologies. It is now commonly stated in development circles that advances in telecommunications and related information technologies offer exciting new possibilities for DOE delivery. DOE schemes that have until recently relied mainly on the mailing of written materials, videos, cassette recordings, and radio or TV broadcasting techniques, can be augmented, enhanced or replaced by new on-line tools and technologies which have the power to transform the learning environment. Several terms are now seen as descriptive of current trends, for example:

— *Convergence*: the coming together of information, communications and media technologies, which promises seamless access to a full range of multi-media resources which educators, students and lifelong learners can use.

— *Wireless and satellite*: the delivery of communications services by new, go-anywhere technologies which also promise lower costs.

— *Leapfrogging*: the opportunity for countries to jump to a new paradigm before problems associated with the delivery of high quality telecommunications or education services have been solved by traditional means.

— *Privatisation & liberalisation*: seen as the twin vehicles for accelerating and facilitating technological advance and access to the wide range of options increasingly available to people living in high income and advanced countries.

Technological developments are coming together which offer the following benefits:

— through the Internet and worldwide web, new and enlarged sources of information and knowledge that offer teachers and students opportunities for self-development as well as benefits from incorporation into classroom environments

— through e-mail and other Internet-related feedback mechanisms, greater opportunity to reduce the isolation and time delay associated with distance education

— through the extraordinary pace of software development, enriched teaching and learning with enhanced graphics, interaction, animation and visualisation

— through lowering telecommunications bandwidth costs and emergence of enhanced cable, wireless and satellite systems, greater opportunities for basic access, video-conferencing, on-line interactive learning, and live interaction with the central place of a distance education programme, and

— through community access schemes, more potential to make the benefits of distance education eventually available to lower income people and rural communities.

Current trends are offering a combination of benefits that will truly improve cost-effectiveness and make DOE an increasingly powerful alternative to the traditional classroom, even in developing countries. Importantly, this combination is also creating an 'education market' in the technology and internet service sectors which will, in turn, increase the level of core funding available from commercial companies who stand to benefit from the demand generated.

The following tables summarise some relevant trends in computers and LANs, the Internet, telecommunications, public access systems and support systems such as electrical power.

Table 1 – Computers & LANs

Category	Trend	Impact
General	Higher operating speeds Lower cost of memory	Pictures, graphics and powerful software packages can be used economically. DE can thus harness ever-improving graphics capabilities to improve interest and acceptability to learners.
PC development and marketing	Rapid pace of development will make more previous generation equipment available to education establishments which can't afford their own.	More equipment availability at marginal cost (this may not be ideal in the rapid paced developed country environment, but could be significant at start-up level in some developing countries).
Software	Enhanced educational software - integrates several elements seamlessly and - offers learners, teachers & administrators control over the learning environment, results, records, etc.	More effectively moderated & controlled DE and learning programmes are possible.
Standards	XML (extensible mark-up language) and IDML (Int'l Development Mark-up Language) will increase database sharing possibilities.	More inter-agency data and experience sharing should improve the rate of development of ICT based distance education.
LINUX operating system	Promises rapid growth	Impact on DE uncertain.

Table 2 – The Internet

Category	Trend	Impact
Growth of Internet	Becoming ubiquitous as a service in urban and sub-urban areas at least, and becoming available in rural areas through various access strategies and technologies	On-line DE techniques available to more and more students and lifelong learners.
Web-site technology	Web based learning becoming widespread	Making incredible amount of information resources, learning management, & student-system interaction available in very user-oriented fashion.
Special access hardware	Low priced internet devices	These will make internet based computer use available to more and lower-income students, and facilitate more devices per classroom and more individualized usage.
Growth of e-commerce	Internet will become increasingly essential to households and communities, and will finance both the internet access, devices & even public access kiosks.	Internet-based DE will have lower marginal access & technology costs. DE products will eventually be marketed on a similar, 'priced & packaged' and deliver basis as other products.
IP Telephony	Better integrated media learning tools will be available through IP systems	Lower costs and greater affordability for all of the long distance communications components of DE.
Desk-top video	Teachers and students can create & exchange real-time or message based talking-head & multimedia materials, without expensive production studio.	Easier and lower cost video-based lesson materials, and non real-time video clips will be sent by email, enhancing contact between teacher and learner.

Table 3 – Telecommunications

Category	Trend	Impact
Radio & wireless	LMDS/LMCS broadband systems provide over-air video and data and/or add two-way features to traditional TV broadcast.	Will provide another, more enriched delivery option for enhanced learning systems to compete with traditional media delivery.
	3G Mobile & fixed-mobile convergence will provide broadband IP access to many sub-urban areas.	Competitive service provision will lower costs and make DE access available on a more mobile or semi-fixed basis.
Existing wire facilities	Digital subscriber loop (DSL)	Will offer higher speed Internet access to more locations including those without cable TV or fibre access.
Satellite	VSAT technology with integrated video and IP applications such as multi-casting.	Opens up remote areas and also provides cost-effective multiple-site networking.
	Digital satellite radio systems will allow agencies to offer radio programmes direct to small handsets anywhere on the globe.	This will facilitate low cost delivery of education programmes globally that have traditionally been delivered only nationally or with lower quality.
	MSS soon to provide voice+64 kbps data, then ultimately bandwidth-on-demand anywhere on the globe.	MSS is a competitive, though probably inferior alternative to VSAT & other geo-stationary satellite techniques for DE purposes.
Network & lesson management products.	Various companies developing integrated systems for open learning networks.	More seamless application of technology. Private telecom & technology companies more involved in the promotion of DE systems and services.
Video transmission	Compression technologies improving.	Allows video to be delivered over a range of telecom facilities.

Table 4 – Publci Access Systems

Category	Trend	Impact
Multi-purpose Community Telecentres (MCCs)	Many pilot systems will result in large number of MCCs, including in rural communities.	Makes computers, internet and email available to low-income people on a community basis.
e-commerce centres	Educational packages and materials could also be accessed on an order and collect basis.	Mass marketing of DE products.

Table 5 – Support Systems

Category	Trend	Impact
Solar power	The unit cost hasn't changed as much as other technologies.	Onus is on technology equipment manu-facturers to reduce their power consumption.
Wind-up systems	Radios, cassette and video players that do not need external power source.	These make technology available to the very lowest income village communities.

Sound pedagogical principles would increasingly dictate the need for a more interactive learning environment which is either difficult to achieve or adds considerably to cost. While satellite improves accessibility to the remotest areas, it was noted that its deployment for this type of delivery requires expensive satellite resources as well as an expensive face-to-face lecture and broadcast system running in parallel. Weaknesses observed were that:

— learners are required to gather at a certain place at a certain time

— learners have no control over the pacing of the broadcast

— broadcasts tend to encourage passivity among learners

— integrating other media is challenging and may lead to inefficient use of the video bandwidth

— broadcasts tend to be organised in time packages that exceed the student's ideal concentration span.

VSAT satellite systems are increasingly seen as a powerful distribution mechanism for Internet-based resources, with ready access to interactive learning tools and e-mail, especially when linked or packaged with key educational web-site sources, servers and services. VSATs can overcome many of the bandwidth/ delivery speed limitations of terrestrial systems, particularly in developing countries, and can be especially economic when deployed in an asymmetric multi-casting mode in which high-speed 'downlink' capability is combined with slower speed 'uplinking.' These features, and the emergence of specially designed DE network management and learner software packages.

The possibilities & pitfalls of harnessing ICTs to accelerate social development. The capacity for VSAT, combined with desk-top video and multi-media tools, facilitating the emergence of relatively low cost video consultation and conferencing. This form of interaction is also utilised effectively for health education, training and remote consultation. It will increasingly become valuable as a means for regional, small centre and rural health development in lower income countries, as international organisations, commercial agencies and eventually governments see the potential and promote its use. It is impossible to offer an exhaustive analysis of which technologies will have the most impact, or to be precise about the most important matters influencing adoption, namely:

— cost: particularly cost per student, cost per graduate, or fixed versus ongoing operational costs, all of which require detailed case-by-case analysis, and

— effectiveness: involving the all-important pedagogical principles, completion successes, etc.

Most of the available material is replete with evidence that the important lessons regarding use of ICTs in distance education are in the early stages of being learned in most countries, and especially in the developing world. In developing countries the educational potential of ICTs is still largely unfulfilled, hence estimating the precise implication of the observable trends for them is hazardous at best.

The use of ICTs in distance education actually depends on at least five factors. These are

— *Geographical size & situation:* Large countries with dispersed people and communities, such as Canada, or island nations such as Fiji or Trinidad & Tobago, have an additional drive or motivation to use communications to deliver some educational services cost-effectively.

— *Policy on telecommunications, the Internet, IT and Education*: Privatisation and liberalisation of telecommunications and the Internet are improving quality, lowering costs and accelerating innovation around the world. Education policy is often key to raising awareness and providing leadership in educational use of ICTs.

— *Population & market size*: Small markets attract fewer investors and less competition, and offer fewer economies of scale which would lead to price reductions, while regional schemes can overcome that, aggregate market size and achieve scale economies.

— *Per-capita income*: The means to address start-up investment challenges and the market affordability to attract commercial players are all-important ingredients to ease the way to change and growth.

— Perceived educational or developmental needs: These can relate to educational delivery challenges due to geographic or cultural isolation, or appreciation for the more systemic challenges – such as adapting to the demands of the information economy which can only be seriously addressed with ICTs.

Many developing countries are facing fundamental problems with education delivery in which ICTs could assist, however they face a severe challenge garnishing the necessary skills and resources to address the opportunity. They may also find difficulty in putting into place a policy environment with which they are entirely comfortable.

Meanwhile high income countries can afford to address a wide range of felt needs; not all their initiatives can be labelled as successes, but such countries can afford to experiment until they get it right. For example, Canada sees a need to address the educational and skills acquisition requirements of its whole labour force in the information age, as well as the special needs of its rural communities, native communities and language minorities. With high national income, forward looking policies, market liberalisation and heavy government investment, it can afford to address the needs and develop new opportunities for its citizens. The dilemma of developing countries is acute. Furthermore, many are justifiably worried that opening to new technology increases their dependency on outside resources. Nevertheless, they will have even fewer options and fall even further behind unless they open their markets sufficiently to improve their Internet access, and adopt policies that encourage the entry of private sector investors and service providers as well as the indigenous use and development of electronic resources.

Policy Environment for ICTs

In this section we will identify and discuss the policy environment which is favourable to the development of the telecommunications and Internet infrastructure, and second how elements of education policy can help the use of ICT in distance education.

Distance education using information and communications technology is, to a large extent, dependent on the reach and quality of a country's existing telecommunications infrastructure. For example, telephone density either limits or allows people to have access to the Internet, and the quality, and capacity of the network determines the potential for DE multi-media applications. Another key condition is the cost of access; high cost telecommunications can severely limit the take-up of DE initiatives.

Effects of privatisation

Privatisation and liberalisation are important steps in the telecommunications sector reform process, resulting in accelerated infrastructure development. Privatisation typically injects needed capital into the sector. In developing countries this often means foreign capital injection. The private investment allows a more speedy network upgrade and roll-out than the state-owned cash-strapped former monopoly operator could accomplish. National policies need not only to privatise their incumbent operators but also ensure that the investment climate is secure and attractive. With privatisation comes a more entrepreneurial and efficient management to the telecom operation.

Introduction of competition is the next step and an important condition for network development. Whereas privatisation brought needed investment to the sector and the efficient management of the operator, competition is the factor that drives the prices down for telecommunications services. Except for Canada which has just recently also opened its local loop market to competition, none of the six case study countries has a fully liberalised telecommunications sector. Ghana created a duopoly by issuing a licence for a private second operator in 1997, but the operator could commence operation only at the beginning of 1999, due to regulatory difficulties. The duopoly expires in 2001. None of the other countries has liberalised their basic fixed service market and only South Africa has provided a fixed date for the liberalisation.

Issues in regulation

Although telecommunications sector reform is called deregulation, it is misleading to think regulation is no longer needed in a liberalised and competitive market, or that the market simply regulates itself. Governments faced with the need to liberalise often fear that national objectives and development goals are neglected by the market, assuming that liberalisation is synonymous with the absence of regulation. This is not the case if effective regulation is in place, as the section below on rural telecommunications will show.

Deregulation means mainly that the government stops influencing the operation of telecommunications networks. Often the ministry responsible for telecommunications is the policy setting body, the regulator and the operator. This needs to end with privatisation and liberalisation.

Effective liberalisation requires an independent regulatory outside of the ministry responsible for telecommunications, since the ministry often still has an ownership interest in the former monopoly operator. The privatisation process usually takes place over several years, with the government retaining a majority or minority share during that period.

A recurrent key problem is that the former monopoly operator uses its market dominance to hinder the new entrant. The regulator's role is to ensure a level playing field and fair competition.

One of the most common problems is the question of interconnection between the incumbent's network and the new entrant. The former monopolist can delay the start in operation of the new entrant through delaying agreement to interconnect arrangements. Competitive service provision is virtually impossible if interconnect is delayed or the interconnection tariffs are overprized and not cost-related.

Rural distance programmes

Distance education is often most needed in rural and remote areas, where it is economically challenging to provide for a small number of residents the same depth and range of education opportunities as cities enjoy. Distance education can enhance and complement local resources. Also, the need for economic development in rural areas makes education all the more crucial.

Unfortunately, in terms of telecommunications infrastructure, rural and poor areas are the most neglected part of the country, making ICT based distance education difficult. Favourable conditions for ICT based distance education can be found in countries that have special programmes for telecommunications network development in rural areas. There is a wide range of possible rural policy plans and actions, some of the most common of which are listed below:

— obligation attached to licenses requiring a certain roll-out target in rural areas

— special rural licenses which are auctioned to the bidder asking for the least subsidy

— the set-up of a rural subsidy fund to supply the above subsidy, levying a small % of revenues from all telecom operators to finance rural network expansion

South Africa is the outstanding example having a very definite policy and institutions to foster access to telecommunications services in rural and disadvantaged communities. In 1996 the government created the unique Universal Service Agency (USA), a statuary body which has the function of promoting, fostering and overseeing the provision of universal access (defined as telecommunications services within walking distance for everybody) and later universal service (affordable individual service).The USA has initiated a telecentre programme to improve access to telecommunications in the country, and a Universal Service Fund (USF) was also. created to help finance the telecentres. The USF receives its money from a levy taxed on all telecom operators, as well as from international donations. In addition, the fixed network operator and the two mobile operators have obligations to provide services to disadvantaged urban and rural areas.

Role of Internet

The Internet plays an important part in ICT based distance education, and most applications are dependent on using the Internet. Therefore, in addition to the policy focused on the telecommunications infrastructure supporting the Internet, the policies and laws directly regulating the Internet have an impact on the potential of ICT based distance education. The following policy principles and regulations are important:

— Liberalisation of Internet Service Providers (ISPs): The majority of countries seem to be following this principle, including developing countries.

— General "hands off" approach towards Internet regulation: This approach recognises the fact that the Internet has developed so rapidly, largely owing to the fact that it was free of hindering regulation. Although still in debate, a view seems to be evolving that the common law should be sufficient to regulate activities on the Internet.

— Promoting broadband and advanced communications: This can be achieved by allowing competition to flourish and the government remaining 'technology neutral.'

— Low import tax on computer hardware and software: This applies also to telecommunications equipment..

— Ensuring that transmission capacity pricing is low and cost-based: Otherwise ISPs cannot offer affordable consumer prices to achieve a mass market.

Similarly crucial is the pricing of local dial-up access to ISPs, which determines the speed of Internet take-up. There is an African policy initiative to guarantee local call prices for access to ISPs nationally, however only 13 countries have thus far subscribed to the concept.

Education policy

From the observation of the six case studies, it seems that the following policy initiatives are important conditions and facilitators of ICT based learning and distance education:

1. *Government awareness of the importance of ICTs for national education*: This demands understanding that

   a) information and communications technology are vitally important to the development of the economy and to participation in the global information society, with a corresponding need to develop appropriate skills, and

   b) ICT based learning and distance education can play a crucial role in broadening access to education for the whole society.

2. *A strategic plan or policy*: This must be based on an analysis of needs and priorities for the use of ICT to improve education. Key elements and concrete steps of such a strategic plan are:

 — ICT skills integration in national curricula

 — equipping schools with computers

 — teacher training on ICT.

 — initiatives and programmes which invite and attract private sector involvement

Two other conditions are important for the success of ICT based distance education. These are

— the presence of local participation and initiative, and

— serious considerations regarding the self-sustainability of projects.

In developing countries the more modest projects are the most successful because they are better able to secure sufficient funding to sustain themselves. The less ambitious and more concrete projects find it easier to secure private sector contributions. The large scale projects are often still in the process of securing and negotiating funding and it remains unclear how operating and recurrent costs will be covered in the long run. In order to develop sustainable ICT based distance education in developing countries, models of financing need to be devised which provide for transition from initial dependency on the international donor agencies to self-sustaining and continuing institutions.

Most rapid progress in policy development seems to be made when various ministries and departments – e.g., telecommunications, industry, human resources and regional development – are all convinced of the need for leadership and co-operate on jointly developing ICT strategy. This reflects common conviction that a policy on ICT in education is just one facet of preparing the population and workforce in all parts of the country to be productive, competitive and at-ease in the information economy.

It is often said that the developing world is in serious danger of falling further behind the advanced world in the information economy. However countries such as India, South Africa, Ghana, etc are making serious attempts to bridge the gulf between the advanced and developing world with the assistance of international organisations. To study in detail let us examine the example of ICT use in distance education programmes of South Africa.

South Africa has a higher urbanisation rate than most of the Sub-Saharan countries. However, some of the huge and disadvantaged townships are included in this urbanisation rate. South Africa, with its history of apartheid, has an outstanding commitment for changing its legacy of inequalities in freedom, access to information, wealth and opportunity based on race. The country is strongly devoted to overcome and mitigate disadvantages for large parts of the society resulting from past policies: Access to information and communications as well as education, freed from the crippling and discriminating concept of Bantu education, are crucial elements and building blocks for the so-called 'empowerment.'

The baseline data gathered on South Africa show the following features of the education situation:

— With gross enrolment ratios of 131%8 for primary and 94% for secondary, it appears that South Africa has successfully managed the delivery of education to these age groups.

— A lower enrolment ratio of 19% can be found in tertiary education, however compared to the U.K.'s 48% with its GNP six times higher than that of South Africa, this seems to be a relatively high enrolment ratio for a middle income country. Within the African Commonwealth countries, South Africa's GNP per capita compares approximately with that of Botswana which has a tertiary enrolment ratio of 6%.

— With nearly a fifth (18%) of the population illiterate, adult education and continuing education are still major issues in South Africa.

Distance education projects in South Africa

In South Africa, the following important projects were identified and used to gain an appreciation of the use of ICT in distance education.

— SchoolNet

— Mamelodi Community Information Services (MACIS)

— Technology Enhanced Learning Initiative of Southern Africa (TELISA)

— Distance Education Digital Learning System (DEDLS) – in planning stage

— the African Virtual University (AVU) – pilot stage completed

— the Universal Service Agencies telecentres

In regards to the focus of those projects there are clearly two concentrations, namely tertiary education and community projects. The African Virtual University, which has just completed its pilot phase, is not only focussed on tertiary education but also on continuing education for professionals from the private sector. The Distance Education Digital Learning System (DEDLS) is still in the planning stage but its first pilot is intended to create content which can be digitally transmitted using different delivery technologies. Its main target audience is post-secondary learners. The third project aimed at tertiary education is the Technology Enhanced Learning Initiative of Southern Africa (TELISA) which already has one ICT centre operating in South Africa. One of its objectives is to improve the access to tertiary education. The TELISA initiative also has a focus on the community: its ICT centres are located or planned in a community setting, serving the needs of the community in general and the business community. One other initiative in South Africa has a major emphasis on the community. The Telecommunications Act of 1996 has established the statutory body of the Universal Service Agency (USA). It is responsible for promoting, enabling and overseeing the provision of universal access to all South Africans, especially those in remote and disadvantaged communities. Universal access is defined as access to a telephone within 30 minutes' walking distance. The Universal Service Agency is using the implementation of telecentres as a major tool to provide universal access to communities.

Telecentres are operated and managed by franchisees which need to be approved by the USA. By fiscal year 1997/1998 it had approved more than 60 telecentres. The Agency has a five-year target which aims to have one. telecentre-type facility in each community (villages, townships, farm community and other) by 2004.

One of the telecentres approved by the USA is the Mamelodi Community Information Services (MACIS). MACIS is run by and situated in a community of around 750,000 residents. Though it was launched in 1995 before the USA had been established, it is now financed by the Agency. SchoolNet South Africa is geared towards providing ICTs for secondary education. As in the school-net in Ghana, some of the schools have acted as ICT centres for their community. In Ghana this was part of the effort to self-sustain the computer labs.

Naturally, ICT based distance education and learning projects provide access to ICT technology and infrastructure. However, the primary goal for some is to provide access to ICT, while for others it is to provide access to certain specific educational content, using ICT as a tool for delivery.

— The primary goal of MACIS and the USA telecentres is to provide access for the community or secondary students to ICT, enabling them to use it to their benefit.

— The AVU, DEDSL and TELISA all aim to broaden the access to specific tertiary education (diplomas, degrees and certificates etc.) by the means of ICT, making ICT access the tool for education delivery, not the main goal.

— SchoolNet features to some extent in the middle, since its main goal is school connectivity but it also stresses online content and curriculum development. Three of the six projects portrayed also have a focus on content production. Similar to SchoolNet, TELISA has a strong focus on content. It plans a series of internet-based information servers in order to provide appropriate support material to existing educational institutions, lecturers, teachers and businesses. One of these servers is already in place: www.africaeducation.org. It is a special web-page for education, development and lifelong learning in Africa. It has not only curriculum content and resources and information on other distance education projects and school projects, but also hosts the 'Africa Digital Library.' It has been available since November 1999 and offers a growing book selection free of charge to African residents.

The planned DEDLS project seems to focus on developing distance education content which is independent of the delivery system as long as it is digitally based. The idea is to develop content which is not produced with a specific medium for transmission in mind but which can be transmitted via a range of alternative technologies.. Within the six initiatives only two were found which specifically included teacher training: the TELISA initiative and SchoolNet SA. Educator training is part of their strategy with the intention to train academic staff and secondary teachers respectively on how to use computers and the Internet for educational purposes.

With an average of 11.46 main lines per inhabitant, South Africa has the highest telephone penetration in Sub-Saharan Africa except for Mauritius. However, there are large disparities between provinces, and between urban and rural telephone penetration. In 1995 the rural telephone penetration was less than half of the urban teledensity. This has since improved significantly, but the disparity is still high. Gauteng and the Western Cape both had a teledensity above 20 per 100 inhabitants in 1995, whereas Mpumalanga, the Eastern Cape, and the

Northern provinces had a teledensity just above 5 per 100 or even below.

With a GNP per capita almost 10 times that of Ghana, and over 36 times that of Mozambique, South Africa also has a computer and Internet penetration many times higher than the other two countries. There are approximately 3.31 Internet users per 100 inhabitants whereas Ghana and Mozambique have just 0.03 and 0.02 respectively. South Africa had 75 Internet Service Providers (ISPs) in 1998 and more than 144,000 Internet hosts, compared to 192 in Ghana and 141 in Mozambique. A huge difference can also be found regarding the PC penetration:

In South Africa the ratio is nearly 5 PCs per 100 inhabitants. Mozambique and Ghana both have a ratio of 0.16 per 100 inhabitants. In traditional media, South Africa has a TV penetration of 12.5 TVs per 100 inhabitants and 20 for radio receivers. The projects can be broadly divided into those which have only user technology in mind and those which also provide or include the infrastructure and transmission technology to deliver education.

Both the AVU and TELISA use satellite broadcasting to deliver education and establish their own transmission facilities. Also, telecentres funded by the Universal Service Agency focus on infrastructure provision to underserved, remote and rural communities, using landlines and cellular technology (the latter through obligations on the two mobile operators, MTN and Vodacom).

Another key infrastructure initiative not portrayed here is Uninet, a provider of national network backbone to its member institutions which are tertiary education institutions, research institutes and some school networks. DEDLS focuses neither on the infrastructure nor on the technology for the end-user, but on digital content packaging, which allows it to be adapted to whatever transmission technology or end-user technology is available. MACIS and SchoolNet focus on equipping the end user, the student and the community with technology and the connection to the infrastructure which provides access to worldwide information. AVU and TELISA, as projects which are more focused on education content delivery than merely on access to IT, both consequently also host information web-pages, providing access to specific information regarding education. MACIS, geared towards the community, includes touch-screen information kiosks, which can be used by computer illiterate people. These examples of ICT based distance education projects illustrate that in South Africa a wide variety of technologies is used to facilitate or deliver education. It seems that there are two determining factors for technology choice:

- the available supporting infrastructure in the country
- the appropriateness for the purpose and end-user of a distance education initiative

Starting with basic statistics, there are two important factors in South Africa which reflect underlying policy decisions and strategy.The 1998 investment in the telecom sector equals approximately 50% of the telecom revenue in the same year, showing a commitment to expand the infrastructure for the future. In 1996, public spending on education was at 7.9% of GNP. In theCommonwealth there are only six countries with higher relative expenditure on education.

The sole fixed-line operator (PTO), Telkom SA, has a five-year period of exclusivity to supply local, national and international telephony, ending in 2002. Telkom has the prospect of a sixth year if it achieves 90% of the five-year total line target by the fourth year of its licence and 80% of its five-year line target. News articles in mid 1999 seem to suggest that it is not likely that Telkom SA will meet the target to obtain an additional year of exclusivity. A second fixed-line operator licence will likely be issued in 2000 or 2001. The second operator will need time to roll out its network in order to come on line as soon as Telkom's period of exclusivity ends in 2002 or 2003..

IIn 1999 there were about 150 ISPs. Approximately 10 are large and more than 120 are 'second-tiered' (virtual ISPs). The 10 'top level' (first-tier) ISPs in South Africa have their own international leased line links.

Telecommunications regulator SATRA ruled that the Internet was in the competitive domain and falls under the Value Added Network Services (VANS) licence, not the voice network licence. This ruling was in response to Telkom's challenge that its monopoly over telecommunications services extended to Internet access. Internet access is provided under a VANS licence under section 40 of South Africa's Telecommunications Act. SATRA has created an Internet regulatory environment based on the following principles:

— universal service obligations on ISPs

— a common 'peering point' (or node), neutrally located and run by a Steering

ISPs in countries which share borders with South Africa benefit from the low tariff policies instituted by the South

African telecom operator for international links to neighbouring countries. As a result, South Africa acts as a hub for some of its neighbours - Lesotho, Namibia and Swaziland.

South Africa has ISPs or local points of presence (POPs) in 70 locations. Unlike the majority of African countries, South Africa has Internet connectivity outside its capital city in most other cities and areas, however there is no low cost local access method in areas outside cities, so the issue of local connectivity is still problematic.

The South African Telecommunications Act No.103 of 1996 provides a summaryof objectives for the regulation and control of telecommunications matters in the public interest. They include

— to promote Universal Service and affordable telecommunications service, including advocacy to raise awareness of telecommunications

— to increase the provision of telecommunication services through rollout and infrastructure provision.

— to promote the innovative development of telecommunications services responsive to consumer/ user needs

— to ensure the needs of local communities and areas are taken into account in relation to the provision of telecommunications services

The Universal Service Agency (USA) is a unique statutory body established by the South African Telecommunications Act of 1996. It will promote affordable Universal Access and Universal Service in Information and Communication Technologies (ICTs) for disadvantaged communities in South Africa to facilitate development, empowerment and economic growth. Its short to medium term objective is to facilitate the provision of telecommunication services where everyone can access them, i.e., within a reasonable distance, which means 30 minutes' travelling. The USA manages a Universal Service Fund (USF) which was established to finance needy telecommunications users in terms of the Telecommunications Act of 1996. A portion of it will be used to subsidise the initial funding of telecentres. The USF is built up by contributions from telecommunications service providers and donor organisations.

The Universal Service Agency launched a Telecentre Pilot Project with the objective of providing universal access to telecommunications in South Africa. These telecentres are managed and operated by approved franchisees and are located in disadvantaged communities, particularly rural areas. The objective of the Telecentre Project is to provide universal access through public facilities: telecommunications, facsimile, e-mail and telephone. Some will provide access to the Internet.

The Agency's aim is to develop a model of how to run telecentres effectively in disadvantaged areas which can then be reproduced, such that they will not need continued funding from the Agency. This will also promote community ownership and control.

All fixed-line and mobile operators have community service obligations laid down in their licences. SATRA has also imposed universal service obligations on ISPs. Among other things, this means that they have to provide services to rural areas. Mobile operators Vodacom and MTN have an obligation to roll out 22,000 and 7,500 community service phones (rural telephones) respectively by 1999. These community service targets were originally put forward by Vodacom and MTN in their licence applications. Phones will operate at a subsidized rate costing approximately 40% of a normal cellular phone call.

Vodacom has franchised members from previously disadvantaged communities to become 'phoneshop' operators in order to provide telecommunication in these communities. MTN has also introduced phoneshops in black townships, consisting of cargo shipping containers with 10 telephone booths installed inside. A third mobile licensee will also be required to provide affordable cellular services to under-serviced areas.

In order to promote universal and affordable service, Telkom SA was granted a period of exclusivity in exchange for stringent rollout dates. The exclusive licence was issued to Telkom in May 1997. Telkom and its strategic equity partners, SBC and Telkom Malaysia, are to double the network in five years. They are particularly required to ensure that villages, schools and clinics receive priority. In order to accelerate the pace of line rollout to fulfil its obligation to provide universal telecommunications service, Telkom introduced its Vision 2000 programme in March 1996.

— Vision 2000 is a five-year network expansion and modernisation programme, where up to 3 million lines will be added to the network (a 75% increase) while another 1 million lines will be replaced.

— Of the 3 million additional lines, an estimated 2 million will be aimed at increasing telephone penetration in under-serviced urban and rural areas, with the remaining 1 million lines catering for growth in developed areas.

The Department of Communications (DOC) has established the Commission for Information Technology (CITA) which will form the initiating platform for public and private partnerships in ICTs, with specific emphasis on creating an Information Technology hub in South Africa. CITA will promote the ideal of a knowledge-based society throughout Africa.

The Department of Arts, Culture, Science and Technology has established a Science and Technology Innovation Fund to support large projects (R1-5 million) in three priority areas, one of which is the development of an information society. In March 1998, the South African cabinet approved a proposal to develop a national information and communication technology strategy. The key elements of the strategy include consolidating all existing government networks in one 'Intranet' and offering the public a 'one-stop shop' through the use of smart cards and public access points. Features of this initiative are:

— Telkom will build the Intranet, which is based on a high-speed fibre optic backbone.

— The public will be able to obtain identity documents and driver's licences as well as information on tenders and health and welfare services through the new system (PITs).

— The Department of Communications will involve various government departments with the aim of preparing legislation for e-commerce, digital signature, multimedia convergence, and encryption.

The former communications minister of South Africa, Jay Naidoo, heralded an intensive public awareness campaign on the evolving information society and the need for information superhighways across the continent. He undertook an 'African Connection Rally' from March-April 1999: this was a 16,000 km journe through Tunisia, Libya, Egypt, Sudan, Ethiopia, Kenya, Tanzania, Malawi, Zambia, Zimbabwe and South Africa, where he visited telecommunication centres in remote areas, inspected facilities, and met with ministers of telecommunications and other government officials. The South African government actively plans, encourages, and supports the development of necessary information and telecommunications infrastructure and has a unique focus and tools for providing telecommunications services to rural and disadvantaged communities.

The Broadcasting Division of South Africa's Department of Communications subscribes also to the vision of establishing an information and knowledge-based society in South Africa. It allocated R1 million at the end of 1998 to provide much needed financial support for broadcasting programmes aimed specifically at the needs of children in the poorer rural areas of the country. It was decided that all funds will initially be concentrated on radio programming and particularly on community radio programmes because of the limited amount of funding available. This project was a huge success and reaffirmed the enormous need for and the positive impact of educational and entertaining community programmes.

South Africa has one public broadcaster, SABC, which has three TV stations, and two private broadcasters. The country is covered by a network transmitting the TV stations, as well as some FW, AM, and shortwave radio stations. The two private broadcasters are MNET and ETV. MNET uses terrestrial and digital satellite broadcasts and its satellite footprints cover large areas of Africa. This operator has also broadcast the TV signals of the three SABC stations since October 1998. ETV is a commercial free-to-air broadcaster that has been awarded the licence to broadcast in South Africa.

There are many small local radio stations all over the country, rendering local service in many indigenous languages. A Community Radio Broadcasting Service, the first in South Africa, was introduced especially to meet the needs of previously neglected rural and disadvantaged communities. The Danish Government Aid Agency (DANIDA) offered to donate R3.1 million for the development of community radio broadcasting with the provision that the South African government match the donation. In response to this, the South African government approved a similar amount to fund the Development of Community Radio Project, which resulted from initiatives taken by the National Community Radio Forum.

By 1996 the Ministry of Education had appointed an investigation team to explore technology-enhanced learning and develop a national strategic plan. Two of the foci were infrastructure and partnerships between the education sector and other stakeholders. Some of the main recommendations of the group were as follows:

— establishment of a clearing house for information on technology-enhanced learning

— inclusion of 'technology-enhanced learning' perspective in teacher development

— integration of IT into national qualifications framework (i.e., school curricula and universities)

— content development

— inclusion of IT in management and administration of education institutions

— co-ordination between ministry and provincial departments

In January 1997 South Africa produced a draft policy document on technology-enhanced learning, setting a framework for planners, decision-makers, administrators and educators. The document recognises the need for enabling conditions and a framework for technology-enhanced education, and it names decision making capabilities and instruments, information, educational infrastructure, physical infrastructure, human capacity and course material as necessary resources.

The outflow of the policy document was a strategic plan, which also concerned itself with funding, and six lead projects which are:

1. curriculum development and delivery in three areas at grade eight
2. technically oriented vocational education in three areas of national priority
3. generic IT course for use in schools, community centres, and other locations
4. development of educators in use of IT for education and training
5. training of managers of learning centres
6. provincial pilot project to test new technologies for education management and administration support Another important policy document on continuing education 11 promotes the concept of an open

learning society and highlights the use of IT, such as the Internet, and the access it provides to learning on the web or to a network of education providers.

Teacher education is sought as a necessary element of the national curricula development for students, outlined and reflected in the national qualifications framework (NQF), the South African Qualifications Authority (SAQA) and new education legislation such as Curriculum 2000. The technology literacy requirements for teachers include certain skills and capabilities for dealing with the information society in which they live, processing of data, and computer literacy including Internet and e-mail. The Department of Education plans and focuses on computer and Internet connectivity for schools, and it works closely with SchoolNet SA.

The review of the policy in the telecommunications and IT field, in media and education demonstrates impressively that in all those areas

— there is an awareness by the government of the issues

— there are national policies and strategies in place aimed at creating favourable conditions, with a huge level of achievement

— the government itself is leading major concrete initiatives

In the case of South Africa, there thus appears to be a well-integrated set of strategies which has resulted in major initiatives, although most are still in relative infancy and results are not easily gauged at this stage. In the country ICT based distance education is sponsored by a range of local organisations and commercial sponsors. Five of the six projects portrayed in this report were initiated by South African organisations (TELISA by Technikon SA, DEDSL by COLISA/ UNISA), by people directly concerned with the issues (SchoolNet SA, MACIS) and the government (Universal Service Agency). The exception is the AVU which is a regional initiative led by the World Bank. Three of the five local initiatives are also sponsored by South African based commercial organisations. The exceptions are the government-led telecentres and DEDLS, which is still in the planning stage. The commercial sponsors range from technology and infrastructure providers to companies in unrelated sectors such as an insurance company and breweries.

The World Bank and the IDRC are each sponsoring three of the projects. Other sponsors are national governments, the EU and a special funding trust for South Africa. International commercial sponsors are all large corporations in the IT field, such as Microsoft, Siemens and many others which are part of the WorLD global partnership, which is involved in SchoolNet SA. South Africa thus possesses the advantage of having strong national leadership, as well as a large potential market, which attracts major corporate interest. The DEDLS initiative has no sponsors yet but is expecting to attract sponsors which are interested in experimenting with the design of a content delivery system and content platforms.

The interests of the MACIS sponsors are focussed around economic development and political empowerment. Sponsors are keen to support the development of the community, provide high quality computer literacy, and foster the creation of employment and employers. The government through the Universal Service Agency is also motivated to support the economic development and empowerment of the people through its telecentres. It is interested in attaining economically sustainable telecentres and focuses its efforts on the least developed communities.

The AVU is a project designed to address two key problems of tertiary education in Africa: lack of access for many students and insufficient quality. It is seen as an innovative way to address these problems. The vision of SchoolNet's sponsors is to create an 'information backbone' of South African Education. The interests of commercial sponsors are understood to be threefold:

— boosting the public image and take part in building the future of the country

— introducing their products to future potential users

— contributing to creation of an educated and computer skilled workforce, thus boosting market size for their products. Similar motivations and interests of sponsors apply to TELISA.

In South Africa -based distance education projects and initiatives flourish and a large number of international donor agencies and agencies involved in distance education are present which initiate or participate in those projects. However, most impressive is the leadership and support of local organisations, education providers and companies in using ICT to deliver and broaden the access to education. The success of so much activity in the ICT-based distance education field can be largely accounted for by an extremely supportive policy environment. In all three areas, telecommunications and IT, media and education, the government has not only formulated policies which clearly identify and determine the role of ICT and education in its future economy and society, but has also created the tools and initiated concrete steps to foster and achieve its goals.

African Virtual University (AVU)

The objective of AVU is to build human capacity and support economic development by leveraging the power of modern information and communications technology to provide world-class tertiary education and training programmes to students and professionals in sub-Saharan Africa. It is a first-of-its-kind interactive instructional telecommunications network. AVU uses interactive satellite and computer-based technologies to make academic. faculty, library resources and laboratory experiences available simultaneously to a network of sites across Africa. Since 1997, AVU has broadcast over 2,000 hours of interactive instruction. More than 9,000 students have completed semester-long courses in the sciences and over 2,000 participants have attended seminars on topics such as e-commerce, accounting and Y2K issues. As of July 1999, the AVU has a digital library that enables users to access thousands of journals from various countries.

The World Bank has provided financing through its Information for Development Programme (InfoDev), the Development Grant Facility (DGF), several Institutional Development Grants, and through the use of a number of IDA credits to African countries. A small core team at the World Bank manages the AVU. The European Union and the governments of Belgium, Canada, Ireland, Norway, Sweden, and the United States have provided funding for AVU. Approximately 30 institutions in North America and Europe, mainly universities and training institutions, have provided course content.

INTELSAT provides AVU with satellite capacity and it had initially, in 1997, sponsored free services. INTELSAT is operated as an international commercial cooperative, with 143 member countries. As a wholesaler of satellite communications, it owns and operates a global communications satellite system providing capacity for voice, video, corporate/ private networks and Internet in more than 200 countries and territories.

The AVU has formed partnerships with 24 universities in 15 sub-Saharan countries. Partner institutions in Africa provide academic, administrative, technical and student support services and infrastructure required to implement AVU operations in-country. Specifically, the three participating universities in Ghana are (a) University of Accra, (b) University of Cape Coast, and (c) University of Science and Technology, while the two participating universities in South Africa are (a) Technikon Southern Africa and (b) University of Pretoria. AVU is supported by international consultants with experience in academic matters, distance learning, library systems, ICT, business planning and marketing.

Main target audience is undergraduate students. Additional audiences are high school students or graduates wishing to enrol in AVU degrees (remedial instruction for students not qualified to enter technical, medical, or scientific fields of study). Professionals from the public or private sector including teachers (continuing education)

AVU's main areas of focus are degree courses in computer science, computer engineering and electrical engineering (currently being developed), IT certificates and courses, language training, and continuing education for professionals from the private sector. AVU offers courses in English and in French. AVU soon plans to offer undergraduate degrees as well as teacher training, executive business education, and IT training.

The technology used include:

— Satellite

— Broadcasting/video

— PC

— Internet AVU website that provides access to e-mail and a digital library.

The pilot phase is currently being evaluated, having been tested in 16 English-speaking and 8 French-speaking African universities in 15 countries, proving the project to be technically and operationally feasible. The 15 participating countries are Ethiopia, Ghana, Namibia, South Africa, Tanzania, Uganda, Zimbabwe, Benin, Burkina Faso, Burundi, Mauritania, Niger, Rwanda, and Senegal.

The AVU was established in 1996. Its pilot phase will be completed in 1999. Preparations are currently underway to launch operational phase (degrees) in 2000. The AVU has plans to expand enrolment by developing further partnerships with local universities, private educational institutions, and business entrepreneurs. The AVU plans to establish up to 200 financially self-sustaining learning centres in the countries of sub-Saharan Africa by 2002.

Total cost of pilot phase (1996-1999) was US$ 12 million. AVU plans to seek additional funding of $10 million for the next development phase in 2000 as well as further sums for its operational phase from a wide range of public and private sector partners. The AVU hopes that the development of further partnerships with private educational institutions and business entrepreneurs will promote the emergence of entrepreneurial private educational centres that will provide financing to AVU through sharing revenues already being generated from tuition fees. The AVU plans to become a non-profit organisation some time in the year 2000 with the involvement of its major stakeholders in Africa and abroad.

Mamelodi Community Information Services (MACIS)

MACIS is a community-based organisation, registered under Section 21 Company Act. Its mission is to provide information on all aspects of life to community members to cope with their normal day-to-day problems and to improve their quality of life. The aim is also to bridge the perception of inaccessibility that surrounds the term 'information' and to introduce information and communication technologies to the community of Mamelodi. The Canadian IDRC is supporting the project through the Universal Service Agency, a statutory body established by South Africa's Telecommunications Act of 1996 to promote universal access to telecommunications for all in South Africa.. The project is situated in a community of around 750,000 residents. There are 40 primary schools, 14 high schools, one university, two technical colleges and one private school. Mamelodi is 22 kilometres to the east of Central Pretoria, in the Gauteng Province of South Africa.

MACIS is the only telecentre in the community. A number of vendors are offering services on a smaller scale, e.g., telephones and fax. Most are telephone shops Initially the project came from the Mamelodi Youth

Organisation in 1986, but they were stopped due to apartheid laws. In 1993 the CSIR (Council for Scientific and Industrial Research) came with a concept of establishing Community-Based Information Services (CBIS). The CSIR targeted Mamelodi to be their pilot location. The idea was discussed with the leaders and a workshop was convened with representatives from youth, women, political parties, religion, education, health, government and other organisations. The project was launched in 1995. The CSIR phased out in 1997 and the project became a community project, run by a board of directors elected by the community, a project manager hired by the board, and some volunteers.

Non-profit providers/ sponsors and area of sponsorship/ donation The World Bank initially sponsored the project through the CSIR. The project is presently sponsored by the IDRC, a Canadian organisation, through the Universal Service Agency. Ithuba Trust, Pretoria Development Trust and Independent Development Trust also funded the project after it became a community project. The Ithuba Trust, Pretoria Development Trust and Independent Development Trust (IDT) are funding organisations in South Africa whose main areas of funding include education, welfare, and health as well as job creation, career guidance, leadership and skills development.

The project created partnerships with Telematics for African Development (TAD), National Information Technology Forum (NITF), IDRC and USA, the CSIR and Mamelodi Planning Zone Forum 4 (PZF4). Planning Zones Forums have been set up by the local government "where stakeholders can come together at grassroots level to consult and inform ward counsellors.".

The major sponsors of the project are: South African Breweries, Siemens sponsors and Telkom SA. The interests of the sponsors have been outlined as community development, computer literacy, and encouragement of a well-informed community that takes part in decision-making on issues that affect their daily lives, identifying their needs and prioritizing them without fear. Local NGOs, Community-Based Organisations (CBOs), the business sector, schools, etc. In South Africa, CBOs may be involved in regional planning in the areas of economic development, education and health intervention.

School children, high school and tertiary students, local business people, professionals, ordinary members of the community are the major audiences.

Technology used by the project include: PC, Internet, touch screen information kiosk, Multimedia CD-Roms, electronic database, a wireless network system called Community Information Delivery System (CiDS) invented by the CSIR to connect to the Internet.

SchoolNet South Africa

SchoolNet SA is a national organisation (NGO) formed to develop and support the implementation of Information and Communication Technologies (ICTs) in schools. It works directly with schools at a provincial level. In early 1998, SchoolNet adopted and began managing the World Bank's World Links for Development (WorLD) project as a lead implementation project in three provinces: KwaZulu-Natal, the Eastern Cape, and North-West. The WorLD project in South Africa is a pilot educational project that aims to introduce ICTs to disadvantaged schools nationwide.

A feature of SchoolNet's model is to build and work through provincial school network structures. In 1998, SchoolNet worked with provincial departments of education and existing or emerging school networks in six provinces, with support to be extended to the remaining three provinces in 1999. SchoolNet and. provincial school networks provide a number of services to schools, including SchoolMail (a low-cost, multi-user e-mail solution), connectivity services, and domain registrations.

SchoolNet's formation emerged from the activities of provincial school networks in four provinces. South Africa's Centre for Educational Technology and Distance Education in the Department of Education agreed to act as co-ordinator for SchoolNet's establishment. SchoolNet has established a partnership with the government and the school networking, NGO and donor communities. This strategically positions SchoolNet to draw on a wide range of resources from different sectors while ensuring that the organisation works within government policy and implementation frameworks. SchoolNet's provincial school networking partners are (a) Western Cape Schools Network; (b) Pretoria Education Network and Gauteng Schools Network, (c) Eastern Cape Schools Network, and (e) Kwa-Zulu Natal Schools Network. These collaborative NGOs were established by groups of schools between 1993 and 1998 to assist fellow schools to connect to and use the Internet.

Besides the school networks, SchoolNet also partners with research organisations and donors, including:

—World Bank Economic Development Institute - World Links for Development (WorLD) programme, which provided initial legal, administrative and financial assistance. As well, the WorLD Programme provides equipment, training and educational support to schools, with the objective of developing participation in collaborative projects and partnerships between schools.

— World Bank - SA Resident Mission, which provided initial direct funding of some programme activities prior to IDRC involvement.

— IDRC ROSA and IDRC Acacia which provided considerable support in the process of SchoolNet's formation as well as initial legal, administrative and financial assistance. Acacia's funding and support extends over two years. SchoolNet SA is housed within the IDRC. The World Bank and IDRC have a bilateral agreement for the WorLD programme, whereby the IDRC will manage WorLD funds for SchoolNet.

Open Society Foundation for South Africa (OSF-SA), which provided initial legal, administrative and financial assistance (funding). OSF-SA was established in 1993 to promote the development of open society in South Africa. To that end, the foundation supports a variety of programmes in the areas of educational, social, legal and health care reform.

SchoolNet SA has formed a number of key private sector partnerships and, in October 1999, funds from the private sector exceeded those from its traditional funding organisations and are key to the project's implementation.

SchoolNet's objective is to assist in the development of a national education network, forming an 'information backbone'. Its programme objectives are towork in the areas of connectivity and technology, human resources development, online content and curriculum support material, and marketing and advocacy. SchoolNet SA seeks to support educators and learners in transforming education through the application of ICTs by providing leadership, expertise and resources. To realize these aims, SchoolNet forges partnerships in the areas of Internet connectivity and relevant technology, content and curriculum development, human resource development and capacity building with various people and organisations that share a common vision.

SchoolNet SA partners with four national government departments which have key stakes in South Africa's education and training system:

— Department of Education's Centre for Educational Technology and Distance Education (CETDE) - it has adopted SchoolNet SA as one of its projects for 1998 and has been involved in SchoolNet SA activities. CETDE provides SchoolNet SA with primary guidance.

— Department of Arts, Culture, Science and Technology

— Department of Communications

— Department of Trade and Industry

The main audience of the project are secondary school students, communities. IDRC Acacia views SchoolNet SA as one of the most successful national school networking initiatives they support. According to Acacia, SchoolNet has been able to make impressive inroads because of South Africa's more established infrastructure and policy environment. Private sector contribution, which is in the millions of Rand, has consisted primarily of in-kind contributions. Initially, the majority of company contributions came from marketing budgets, but increasingly large portions of money are coming core development and strategic funding. It is thus anticipated that contributions from the private sector will continue to increase dramatically.

IDRC/Acacia is providing funding of CAD $472,000 for two years. The funding supports three staff positions, support costs, a connectivity programme in four provinces, and other activities in support of SchoolNet's aims and objectives. It will also provide equipment and connectivity to at least 48 schools as well as eight training workshops.

The Open Society Foundation for South Africa (OSF-SA) provided an 18-month grant of R755,000. This supports one position as well as associated programme grant to further SchoolNet's work in the area of online content and curriculum resource material and working with the OSF's programmes in the Northern Province and Eastern Cape. The OSF approved the grant on 10 June 1998. In addition to the IDRC and OSF funding, SchoolNet is indirectly supported through its role as implementer of the WorLD programme, which contributes a staff member as project manager, as well as associated local programme funding of approximately R320,000 annually.

Technology Enhanced Learning Initiative of Southern Africa (TELISA)

The TELISA initiative aims to facilitate the establishment of a number of Information Technology (ICT) Centres throughout the sub-region of the Southern African Development Community (SADC) and a series of

Internet-based information servers to provide appropriate support material to existing institutions, lecturers, teachers and businesses. TELISA currently has ICT centres in Lesotho and South Africa. ICT Centres will promote lifelong learning, telemedicine, safety and security in a community setting. A grant was provided by Technikon SA to establish three ICT Centres in three South African provinces: Mpumalanga, Eastern Cape, and Free State. Technikon SA regional directors, in co-operation with local business and community structures, will run the centres on a self-sustainable basis. The Kgautswane ICT Centre in Mpumalanga Province, South Africa was officially opened in October 1999. An ICT Centre in Lesotho was opened 5 March 1999.

TELISA has also enabled a special web-page for education, development and lifelong learning in Africa: www.africaeducation.org. This is their information server, also called an information clearing house. Besides information and access to curricula content resources, other distance education projects and school projects, it offers the Africa Digital Library. The digital library has been available free for residents of Africa since November 1999 and offers a growing digital book selection (around 3-4,000 currently). TELISA has a focus on three components of distance education: affordable infrastructure, access for learners, and content.

The Centre for Lifelong Learning (CLL) of Technikon of Southern Africa (SA). Technikon SA is a technology/ polytechnic university that specializes solely in distance education. This has been and is still mainly based on print material, but they are shifting to new technologies. Technikon SA has approximately 80,000 students per year and is funded partly by the government and partly through student fees. Technikon

SA funds TELISA through external funds. Technikon has regional offices throughout South Africa.

Established in 1993 by Technikon of Southern Africa, the CLL seeks to promote non-formal education through programmes custom designed at Technikon. The Centre operates in collaboration with all academic programme groups that are able to support the Centre's programmes and a range of outside organisations. The Centre has a small, full-time staff complement and contracts staff where necessary for specific projects.

Technikon SA is the most substantial sponsor of TELISA with approximately US$ 200,000 from their strategic reserve towards the ICT centres. Technikon SA also sponsored US$ 120,000 for the initial establishment of the African Digital Library. World Bank (Africa Sector) sponsored US$ 50,000 toward the cost of the computer system as well as training and support of the Kgautswane ICT Centre..

Safmarine company is a local shipping company which provided used shipping containers for the Kgautswane ICT Centre. Those were remodelled to build rooms and offices for the ICT Centre. The Old Mutual Company is a large South African insurance company which supported the Centre. Old Mutual contributed financially and with technical support to the Kgautswane community. Daimler-Chrysler sponsored US$ 54,000 for the ICT Centre in Lesotho.

According to its vision and mission statement, the Centre for Lifelong Learning (CLL) is committed to promoting awareness of educational opportunities, improving access to tertiary education, and serving the expressed and dormant needs of the business community, the community in general, and disadvantaged learners in particular. CLL is interested in providing a life-long, career-orientated educational path for learners from all walks of life.

Technikon SA had discussions with members of the following organisations to plan the TELISA initiative:

— The Distance Education Association of Southern Africa (DEASA)

— The Telematics for African Development (TAD) Consortium

— UN Economic Commission for Africa (Food, Safety and Security) - UN ECA

— SADC HR Development Co-ordinating Office (Swaziland)

— P.E.A.C.E. Foundation

— The Centre for Educational Technology and Distance Education (South Africa's Department of Education)

— Universal Services Agency of South Africa

The Kgautswane ICT Centre is located in the deep rural area between the towns of Lydenberg, Ohrighstad and Burgersfort. The area reaches into both the Northern Province and the Mpumalanga Province. The immediate area of Kgautswane has a population of approximately 60,000 people. It has no piped. water or electricity, few roads, and little industry/ business. The nearest post office and photocopier were approximately 28 km from the Centre.

The CLL provides services in the following areas:

— teaching to the community and business community and offering capacity-building programmes by means of contact, participation, and distance education

— researching the needs, relevance and efficiency of CLL programmes, including the research generated by students and course participants

— facilitating and contributing to community-based initiatives aimed at the enhancement of the community in general.

Most centres will likely comprise 10 PCs, a server, telephones and a range of work-station equipment to support business and learner needs. This includes Internet, e-mail, and shareware programmes to access the Internet. As well, ICT Centres typically have payphones, fax machines, scanners, photocopiers, typing services, community information and document lamination.

Technikon also established a satellite reception area to receive programmes broadcast from C-Band satellites. A second reception centre is planned for installation during December 1999/January 2000 in Port Elizabeth, South Africa. This will be equipped with a sub-centre having two workstations some 10 km away and it will be run and based by the regional office of Technikon SA. It will have a satellite reception facility and receive programmes from the African Virtual University (AVU). The 10 PCs at the main centre plus the two remote PCs will all have Internet access.

The Kgautswane ICT Centre received a grant to get started, but is now charging for services to sustain itself. It is not geared for commercial operation, but to be run by the community. This means that it is required to generate enough revenue to cover all running and upgrade costs. Also the information server on African education and the African Digital Library are designed to sustain themselves. The web-page will use advertising to cover its cost. The cost of domain registration was covered by the CLL Director, and a grant from TSA covers some of the costs of a staff member who assists with finding learning content on the Internet.

The African Digital Library offers companies to sponsor the purchase and digitalization of books. The library books are provided in encrypted format allowing only one user to access each purchased book at the same time. Additional copies of eBooks or their print equivalents may be purchased via an e-commerce interface provided by netLibrary.

Open Distance Learning (ODL) system for Africa

The Distance Education Digital Learning System (DEDLS) project is currently in its conceptual design phase. The project aims to provide quality distance learning and student support particularly for students in remote areas in Africa. The project is unique because it seeks to "establish the next paradigm for distance education." Africa's limitations with existing communication technologies and traditional delivery systems have necessitated a solution that leapfrogs previous eras of technology. The pilot is seen as a stepping stone for the foundation of the 'African Digital University.'

The project's first pilot will develop 10-15 hours of distance learning content that can be delivered using multiple 'digitally-based' delivery alternatives: print, compressed video, audio and electronic interaction. The pilot will also demonstrate the feasibility and sustainability of one or a network of mobile or fixed telecentres to deliver tertiary distance education (DE) and to provide student support in remote areas of Africa. Initially, one mobile telecentre will undergo limited testing in remote rural areas. Mobile telecentres will have their own power-generating capabilities and a range of ICT equipment. The telecentres are to be managed and operated by small business entrepreneurs in the community in such a way that teaching and digital student support is provided at no extra cost to the learner. One of the projected outcomes of the pilot is to demonstrate financial sustainability of the model and to develop the corresponding business plans.

The dominant target group is post-secondary learners in rural and urban township environments. However, once the systems are developed and digital learning centres are operational, the project is envisaged to have application potential for secondary, preschool and basic adult education.

The University of South Africa (UNISA) is the lead agency and initiator, but the pilot project will be conducted under the auspices of COLISA (Confederation of. Open Learning Institutions of South Africa, including Technikon South Africa, UNISA and Vista University). The pilot project will include participation from SAIDE (South African Institute of Distance Education – regional DE NGO), CSIR (Centre for Scientific Research) and is being conducted in consultation with the World Bank. These members will form part of the core project team.

The project's leading participants (see section B above) are currently in the process of approaching the donor community for funding of the pilot. The project is currently being introduced to the donor community as a COLISA project regarding funding of the pilot. The pilot is estimated to cost approximately $350,000. D) Commercial providers/ sponsors and area of sponsorship / donation A global approach is being planned for an alliance among governments, the private sector and public education providers, from the African continent and worldwide. The primary motivation for sponsors is the development of a continental open digital learning system that is capable of reconfiguring knowledge according to specific developmental needs and delivering this in a sustainable way to rural communities in Africa. There are also many contextual factors that have driven the initiative, including the challenge of improving DE pedagogy and student support, the challenge of diminishing resources in higher education and increased competition in the DE sector. There are plans to involve the Economic Commission for Africa, one of the UN bodies. The lead agency is currently working in close consultation with the World Bank.

The plan is to focus on structured degree, diploma and certificate programmes rather than a wide-ranging open choice of subject fields. However, because the system is based on a digitised knowledge domain, it will be technically possible to customise choice of content for individual learners. The plan is also to focus on critical areas such as the sciences, training for good governance, and financial and business training. The intention is to design the system in such a way that it would be capable of teaching using technologies including radio, broadcasting/video, PC, Internet, multimedia CD-Roms, electronic databases, satellite, wireless, etc. The idea is to be able to respond quickly to existing and new infrastructures within Africa.

Universal Service Agency – Franchised telecentres

The Universal Service Agency (USA) launched a Telecentre Pilot Project with the objective of providing universal access to telecommunications (defined as within 30 minutes' walking distance) in South Africa. These telecentres are managed and operated by approved franchisees and are located in disadvantaged communities, particularly rural areas. The objective of the Telecentre Project is to provide universal access to telephones, facsimile and e-mail. Some will provide access to the Internet.

Besides providing telecommunications, many telecentres will also provide other services such as small business support, health, education and training. Some may offer a range of services from telemedicine to telelearning and telelibraries. There is also a plan to link these telecentres directly to both government and private databases around the country in the near future. By the 1997-1998 fiscal year, the Agency had approved 68 telecentre applications throughout the country, including six pilot telecentre communities. Telecentres are funded by the Universal Service Fund (USF).

The responsibility of managing a telecentre lies with the franchisee, not the Agency. The Agency aims to develop a model of how to run telecentres. effectively and to be self-sustaining in disadvantaged areas; this can be reproduced, and it will also promote community ownership and control.

The USA is the initiator and lead agency. It is a statutory body established by the South African Telecommunications Act of 1996. The Agency will subsidise the least developed communities, individuals and organisations in acquiring telecentres. The Agency may provide capital or start-up funding to equip telecentres with telephones, a printer, a fax machine, a photocopier, and computers.

3

Instructional Tools for Distance Education

Distance education programmes can be enriched and made more attractive, effective and satisfying by using a variety of media relevant to the content for learning and the facilities that can be provided should attempt an exploitation of the potential of the variety of powerful media provided by modern technology. The present day mechanical devices have brought about a virtual revolution in diverse field of human activity. A variety of instructional tools in distance education in open universities as well as in institutes of distance learning are described in this chapter.

The media used for distance education can be classified into two groups: print media and non-print media. Distance education cannot do without printed course material. It is the mainstay of the instructional system almost everywhere. It is in the form of reading material or in the form of programmed instructional material. It is the most popular medium because it is easy to carry, is comparatively cheaper and can be used according to the convenience of the learners. The learners get the self- instructional material at their homes by post. The material is carefully prepared by experts in the field of their expertise to suit the needs of the learners and to help them learn the subject without much assistance from others. The area of non-print media includes the technologies such as radio and television, telephone, videotex, computers, internet, satellites and so on.

— *Radio:* Radio is being increasingly used in advanced countries to overcome the shortage of qualified teachers and suitable books. It can enrich the farthest corners. If the radio has become a necessary instrument of education in advanced and progressive countries, the services it can render are still far greater in a country like India. As a matter of fact, the radio is an effective medium and has been extensively used for educational purposes to spread literacy or to give formal or non-formal education all over the world. In addition to the printed materials lessons are planned and written for broadcast from All India Radio. Radio programmes supplement and reinforce instruction imparted through the printed material.

— *Television*: Television is a more effective medium than radio for spreading education, because the language of TV is rich, powerful and expressive. TV lessons are entertaining as well as attractive. A lesson received through the gates of eyes and ears has a double chance of retention by learners.

— *Audio-video cassettes:* The audio/video cassettes can be played and replayed at home by the learner at his/ her will. A learner can stop a particular tape at a point where more details are necessary and can play in slow motion to understand a difficult point. He need not get up early in the morning or wake up late in the night for radio and TV broadcasts. The use of video enabled a good lecturer to be seen and heard all over the country, without having to repeat his performance. At the moment, the video equipment is costly in India and even in other developing countries and they are not within the reach of most of the students.

— *Telephone:* The telephone is a very effective means of communication. It offers two ways interactive communications across distance, i.e., people can talk to each other, discuss and ask questions. In India this is unlikely to be considered as a medium in distance education.

— *Videotex:* The videotex makes home television sets to function like a computer terminal and retrieve text information and graphics from a remote database. It gives much wider access to information and much wider ease with which new concepts and ideas can be transmitted.

— *Computers*: The mass teaching system has become virtually impossible without a computer. The computer is a very good tool to improve the process of teaching and learning. It is of tremendous use for teaching and learning in diverse situations. Computer based instructions include a broad range of applications. The major classification of computer application for distance learning are "Computer Assisted Instruction and Computer Management Instruction". The target number of students must be large because of the special skills and time required to develop effective computer-aided instruction.

— *Internet*: The internet is the largest, most powerful computer network in the world. It encompasses 1.3 million computers with internet addresses that are used up by 30 million people in more than fifty countries. As more colleges, universities, schools, companies and private citizens are connected to the internet either through affiliations with regional not-for-profit network or by subscribing to information services provided for profit companies, more possibilities are open for distance educators to overcome time and distance to reach students. The easy availability of computers and worldwide internet has brought about significant changes in learning-teaching strategies. The present electronic communication system has made the interaction much easier and essentially less costly. With the access to internet, distance educators and their students can use the Electronic Mail (E-Mail), Bulletin Boards and World Wide Web (WWW). The WWW and web browsers have made the internet a more user-friendly environment.

— *Satellite*: The satellite is the glamourous medium in distance education. It is used for communicating over long distance. More channels for both radio and television are possible because of the satellite. Programmes are viewed by people in cities as well as in countryside locations. The satellite and television network offers a powerful medium for the dissemination of knowledge, cultural programme and developmental information. A wide area is covered without any loss of quality in the messages sent. The communication channels are not affected by natural calamities as is usually the case with telephone wires. All teaching and learning programmes can be greatly improved by visual and auditory materials because these make the learning experience far more concrete and memorable. But the media has remained under-exploited by the distance learning system for want of appropriate and relevant software which is the greatest problem of this system.

In distance learning students and teachers will find themselves playing different roles than is the norm in traditional education. The teacher is no longer the sole source of knowledge but instead becomes a facilitator to support student learning, while the student actively participates in what and how knowledge is imparted. More than any other teaching method, distance learning requires a collaborative effort between student and teacher, unbounded by the traditional limits of time, space, and single-instructor effort. Advances in telecommunications technology has opened up the possibility of personal and group interaction in distance education. Both computer and audio conferencing permit the introduction of class discussions without the group meeting face to face. Phone calls and electronic mail replaces personal office visits. The distance learner can now have almost the same instructional contact and interaction as the student on campus.

Major instructional tools for distnce education are discribed below in detail.

Instructional Television (ITV)

ITV is an effective distance education delivery system that can be integrated into the curriculum at three basic levels:

1) *Single lesson:* Programs address one specific topic or concept, providing a lesson introduction, overview, or summary.

2) *Selected unit:* A series of programs providing the content foundation for a learning unit in the course curriculum.

3) *Full course:* Programs from one or more ITV series may be integrated into a full semester course typically in conjunction with instructional print materials.

ITV may be either passive or interactive. Passive ITV typically involves pre-produced programs which are distributed by video cassette or by video-based technologies such as broadcast, cable, or satellite. In contrast, interactive ITV provides opportunities for viewer interaction, either with a live instructor or a participating student site. For example, two-way television with two-way audio allows all students to view and interact with the teacher. At the same time, cameras at remote sites allow the teacher to view all participating students. It is also possible to configure the system so that all student sites may view one another.

In designing instruction for ITV, the challenge is to think in visual terms. Taking advantage of the visual imagery of ITV can counter an over-reliance on lecturing. Carefully planning ways to show instead of tell may improve the instructional effectiveness of ITV.

Because teachers and students are physically separated by a distance, the teacher's challenge is to psychologically reduce the gap not only through the appropriate use of technology but also through the use of effective teaching practices. Good teaching ensures that a rapport develops between students and teacher. Once basic teaching methods are considered, try employing the following three step strategy for conducting ITV lessons:

— Remember that it takes longer to deliver instruction at a distance than in a traditional face-to-face setting. Plan lessons accordingly.

— Practice in front of a live camera prior to class. If possible, have a colleague, a few target students, or a media technician view your presentation and on-camera presence, offering suggestions for improvement.

— Organize all class materials and visuals before the start of the class. It is best to have a trial run with technical staff so that all participants know the role they are expected to play.

— If using an overhead camera to electronically project visuals, understand its operation and limitations prior to the start of the class.

— Prepare viewers for new terminology to be used in the program, and answer any questions regarding the technical equipment being used, such as cameras, television monitors, audio equipment, etc..

— Inform students if there will be camera operators or technicians in the classroom. Although the students may be initially curious, this will fade as the class progresses. In-class technicians are trained to be as unobtrusive as possible.

— Students should have the necessary background materials to make the best use of televised lessons. Consider the use of study questions to assist in focusing discussions.

— Consider team teaching to maintain viewer interest with a change of voice, image, and presentation style. If using guest speakers, give students necessary background information prior to the class. Do the same for the guest speakers. Let them know the specific purpose of their session, what is expected of them, and the general background of participating students.

— Vary facial expressions, tone of voice, body movements, and eye contact with the camera to enhance verbal communication.

— Engage students by using humor, asking questions, involving students, and praising student contributions.

— Maintain energy and dynamism to attract and hold the distant learners' attention. Remember, enthusiasm is contagious. So is boredom.

— Present content in five to ten minute blocks interspersed with discussion. Alternate between instruction and interaction.

— Keep lecture sessions simple and clear. To help focus viewing, indicate key points to look for.

— Do not read material.

— Maintain a moderate speaking pace.

— Do not digress — keep students on track.

— Include different kinds of student involvement—watching, reading, writing, and talking.

— Vary the center of focus for activities from the on-camera presenter to a receive site group or individual.

— Incorporate timely breaks as a respite from the television monitor.

— Motivate peer learning and support by encouraging students to work together both in and out of class.

— Review the concepts discussed in the program and clarify any misunderstandings by asking focused questions.

— Integrate activities to reinforce the content presentation. These activities might include quizzes, worksheets, role-playing, and experiments.

— Planning a block of time for interaction and then letting students know in advance that interaction is anticipated. Initiating an interaction within the first twenty minutes will get students motivated to participate in learning rather than lulling them into just watching.

— Designating students at distant sites to lead discussions or survey the room for questions.

— Clearly defining discussion topics or questions and then allowing time for students to prepare responses. Assigning discussion questions in advance of the television session will help students prepare for the interaction.

— Encouraging student-to-student interaction by asking an in-class student or a student from a distant site to respond to questions. The instructor does not always have to answer questions.

— Functioning as content facilitator not just content provider.

— Review the taped recordings of the presentation, either with technical staff, a colleague, or by yourself. Take notes for improving presentation, style, and delivery methods.

- Seek student feedback on the strengths and weaknesses of the instructional materials and the teaching strategies being used.
- Be open to new ideas and delivery techniques for improving instructional effectiveness.

Advantages

- Since most people have watched television, the medium is familiar.
- Motion and visuals can be combined in a single format so that complex or abstract concepts can be illustrated through visual simulation. The old cliche "a picture is worth a thousand words" rings true.
- Instructional television is an effective way to take students to new environments (the moon, a foreign country, or through the lens of a microscope).
- Time and space can be collapsed, so that events can be captured and relayed as they happen.
- It is very effective for introducing, summarizing, and reviewing concepts.
- It can be used effectively as a motivational tool.

Disadvantages

- Broadcast quality ITV is expensive to create.
- Video production is time consuming and can be technically demanding, often requiring relatively sophisticated production facilities and equipment.
- Sites choosing to interactively participate in an ITV program may require specialized equipment, facilities, and staffing.

— Most prepackaged ITV courses use a mass media approach to instruction aimed at the average student. As a result, they can be ineffective in serving students with special needs.

— When used passively, without interaction, its instructional effectiveness can be limited.

— Unless professionally produced, completed ITV programs often look amateurish.

— Once completed, ITV programs can be difficult to revise and update.

Interactive Videoconferencing (IV)

IV is an effective tool that may be used in distance education settings. This system can be integrated into the distance education program with minimal adaptation to the curriculum and course and is designed to support two-way video and audio communication between multiple locations.

Most IV systems utilize compressed digital video for the transmission of motion images over data networks such as high capacity Integrated Services Digital Networks (ISDN). The video compression process decreases the amount of data transmitted over the lines by transmitting only the changes in the picture. By minimizing the bandwidth required to transmit the images, video compression also reduces the transmission cost. Interactive videoconferences are often transmitted on dedicated T-1 phone lines. These high speed lines are very effective for videoconferencing, but they are typically leased circuits with an expensive monthly cost. The fixed monthly charge is usually based on distance, not usage.

The cost effectiveness of IV systems increases with use. Interactive videoconferencing systems can operate at different data rates, at various fractions of T-1 capacity, enabling the transmission of multiple simultaneous videoconferences over the same T-1 circuit. An IV system can also share a T-1 circuit with other digital data uses such as Internet transmissions or file transfers.

Interactive videoconferencing is commonly used to connect two locations using sophisticated computer technology. The core of IV is the codec (coder/decoder). This is the electronic device that transmits and receives the video signals that the class members will see on their television monitors. It may be easier to think of the codec as an extremely sophisticated modem.

A modem takes digital data and transmits it over regular phone lines. The codec takes analog signals, compresses and digitizes them, and transmits the signals over digital phone lines. Other types of equipment, such as television monitors, are needed to make IV successful. In addition, various forms of instructional technology can be incorporated into IV, including video cassette recorders/players, microphones, cameras, and computers.

Some systems are also capable of simultaneously connecting more than two sites through the use of a multi-point control unit, or MCU. Multi-point conferencing can be effective although the scheduling, technical, and logistical dimensions of MCU conferences can be imposing.

A relatively new "dial out" feature, allows the use of multiple telephone lines to connect two or more sites in the same conference. Simultaneously accessing multiple lines may be difficult in small areas. In addition, the cost of the telephone line usage may be prohibitive since the cost of the call would be multiplied by the number of lines utilized in the conference.

There are mainly 3 type of of videoconferencing systems. they are:

1) *Small room videoconferencing.* This system is designed primarily for small groups at all sites seated around a conference table.
2) *Classroom videoconferencing.* This type of system usually uses high quality AV components, codecs, and an interface that allows all participants to be seen on the monitors.
3) *Desktop videoconferencing.* This system utilizes a personal computer and videoconferencing software. These systems are less expensive, but offer limited resolution. They are most effective for individual and small group use.

When designing instruction to be delivered over IV, the instructor should focus attention on all students, not just those at the "home" site. Lessons should incorporate a variety of activities for all students at the various sites. Use small group activities, student presentations, and an occasional break to add variety to the lesson.

As a rule of thumb, instructors should change instruction methods every 10-15 minutes. In other words, switch from lecture to question-answer to small group activity on a regular basis. It is often helpful to bring guest lecturers into the classroom. It may also be helpful to have guest speakers at one or more of the distant sites.

This will encourage involvement of the distant students, as well as allowing the students at the origination site to "see what it is like" to have the teacher at another location. When preparing class visuals, keep in mind that small fonts and light colors do not show up well over the monitors. A variety of formatting will also assist in maintaining student interest and attention. When formatting visuals, be sure that they will fit on the television monitor.

Instructional strategy include the following steps

1) *Establish Class Expectations*: In the distance education classroom, some students may adopt the "TV" attitude, expecting the course to be entertaining, not educational. Address this attitude through well planned and focused presentations with emphasis on teacher-student interaction.

2) *Reduce Distractions*: Students should also be forewarned to minimize extraneous noise and activity. Both detract from the quality of the course.

3) *Use Variety and Interaction*: The instructor should begin the course by preparing the learners for an active experience. Interactive videoconferencing is interactive, unlike regular television, and students can make the class much more interesting by being actively involved.

4) *Encourage Dialogue*: By asking questions and noting body language, instructors can ascertain the interest and comprehension of the students at both all sites. This kind of attention will make all students feel more comfortable.

5) *Training for Instructors and Students*: It is important that an instructor be taught how to use all features of the equipment. A short session (30 minutes) should be sufficient to give the instructor a "hands-on" overview of the equipment features. It would also be helpful to provide the instructor with a quick reference sheet outlining major functions.

Some institutions have technicians who will assist the instructor in setting up or monitoring the videoconference. However, the instructor should still be aware of the process because the technician may not always be available. Student training may also be critical since they may be called upon to operate the equipment if the instructor is at another site, is unavailable, or if a guest speaker needs assistance.

Interactive videoconferencing can be an effective instructional tool for the distance educator. As with other technologies, its usefulness is directly related to the instructor's understanding of its benefits, limitations, and utilization strategies.

Advantages

Interactive video can be effective because it:

— Allows "real time" visual contact between students and the instructor or among students at different sites.

— Supports the use of diverse media. Blackboards, handwritten documents, and videos may be incorporated at all sites.

— Enables connection with experts in other geographical locations.

— Can provide access to at-risk or special needs students.

— Provides additional access to students at remote sites.

Disadvantages

Interactive video has the following limitations:

— The initial cost of the equipment and leasing the lines to transmit conferences may be prohibitive.

— Companies which produce codecs have each developed unique methods of compression which are incompatible, although protocols have been established to allow communication among brand names.

— Unless a strong effort is made by the instructor, students not located with the instructor may remain uninvolved in the course.

— If visuals, like handwritten or copied materials, are not properly prepared, students may have a difficult time reading them.

— If the "pipe" that carries the transmission among sites is not large enough, the students may observe "ghost images" when rapid movement occurs in "real time".

— If the system is not properly configured, class members may observe an audio "echo" effect. The result is audio interference that detracts from the learning environment.

Computers

Educators have witnessed the rapid development of computer networks, dramatic improvements in the processing power of personal computers, and striking advances in magnetic storage technology. These developments have made the computer a dynamic force in distance education, providing a new and interactive means of overcoming time and distance to reach learners. Computer applications for distance education fall into four broad categories:

1) *Computer Assisted Instruction (CAI)* - uses the computer as a self-contained teaching machine to present discrete lessons to achieve specific but

limited educational objectives. There are several CAI modes, including: drill and practice, tutorial, simulations and games, and problem-solving.

2) *Computer Managed Instruction (CMI)* - uses the computer's branching, storage, and retrieval capabilities to organize instruction and track student records and progress. The instruction need not be delivered via computer, although often CAI (the instructional component) is combined with CMI.

3) *Computer Mediated Communication (CMC)-* describes computer applications that facilitate communication. Examples include electronic mail, computer conferencing, and electronic bulletin boards.

4) *Computer-Based Multimedia-* HyperCard, hypermedia, and a still-developing generation of powerful, sophisticated, and flexible computing tools have gained the attention of distance educators in recent years. The goal of computer-based multimedia is to integrate various voice, video, and computer technologies into a single, easily accessible delivery system.

Advantages

— Computers can facilitate self-paced learning. In the CAI mode, for example, computers individualize learning, while giving immediate reinforcement and feedback.

— Computers are a multimedia tool. With integrated graphic, print, audio, and video capabilities, computers can effectively link various technologies. Interactive video and CD-ROM technologies can be incorporated into computer-based instructional units, lessons, and learning environments.

— Computers are interactive. Microcomputer systems incorporating various software packages are extremely flexible and maximize learner control.

— Computer technology is rapidly advancing. Innovations are constantly emerging, while related costs drop. By understanding their present needs and future technical requirements, the cost-conscious educator can effectively navigate the volatile computer hardware and software market.

— Computers increase access. Local, regional, and national networks link resources and individuals, wherever they might be. In fact, many institutions now offer complete undergraduate and graduate programs relying almost exclusively on computer-based resources.

Disadvatages

— Computer networks are costly to develop. Although individual computers are relatively inexpensive and the computer hardware and software market is very competitive, it is still costly to develop instructional networks and purchase the system software to run them.

— The technology is changing rapidly. Computer technology evolves so quickly that the distant educator focused solely on innovation "not meeting tangible needs" will constantly change equipment in an effort to keep pace with the "latest" technical advancements.

— Widespread computer illiteracy still exists. While computers have been widely used since the 1960's, there are many who do not have access to computers or computer networks.

Students must be highly motivated and proficient in computer operation before they can successfully function in a computer-based distance learning environment.

Internet

The Internet encompasses 1.3 million computers with Internet addresses that are used by up to 30 million people in more than fifty countries. As more and more colleges, universities, schools, companies, and private citizens connect to the Internet either through affiliations with regional not-for-profit networks or by subscribing to information services provided by for-profit companies, more possibilities are opened for distance educators to overcome time and distance to reach students.

With access to the Internet, distance educators and their students can use:

1) *Electronic mail (e-mail):* Like postal mail, e-mail is used to exchange messages or other information with people. Instead of being delivered by the postal service to a postal address, e-mail is delivered by Internet software through a computer network to a computer address.

2) *Bulletin boards:* Many bulletin boards can be accessed through the Internet. Two common public bulletin boards on the Internet are USENET and LISTSERV. USENET is a collection of thousands of topically organized newsgroups, covering everything from supercomputer design to bungee cord jumping, and ranging in distribution from the whole world to single institutions. LISTSERV also provides

discussion forums on a variety of topics broken out by topic or area of special interest.

3) *World-Wide Web (WWW):* The WWW is an exciting and innovative front-end to the Internet. Officially WWW is described as a "...wide-area hypermedia information retrieval initiative aiming to give universal access to a large universe of documents". The WWW provides Internet users with a uniform and convenient means of accessing the wide variety of resources (pictures, text, data, sound, video) available on the Internet. Popular software interfaces, such as Mosaic and Netscape, facilitate navigation and use of the WWW. The central organizing feature of the WWW is the "home page". Every organization and even every individual user of the WWW can create a home page that contains whatever information they want to present.

The Internet and WWW to help students to gain a basic understanding of how to navigate and take full advantage of the networked world into which they will be graduating. Some instructional possibilities of the Internet include:

— Using e-mail for informal one-to-one correspondence. Feedback from the instructor can be received more quickly than messages sent by mail. Students can read messages at their convenience and easily store them for later reference.

— Establishing a classroom bulletin board. Distant students often work in isolation without the assistance and support of fellow students. Setting up a class bulletin board can encourage student-to-student interaction. With a class computer conference, individual students can post their comments or questions to the class, and every other individual is free to respond. The conference can also be used to post all modifications to the class schedule or curriculum, assignments/tests, and answers to assignments/tests.

— Engaging students in dialogue with other students, faculty, and researchers by encouraging them to join a bulletin board(s) on topic(s) related to the class.

— Developing a classroom home page. The home page can cover information about the class including the syllabus, exercises, literature references, and the instructor's biography. The instructor can also provide links to information on the WWW that would be useful to students in the class.

When incorporating the Internet into a distance delivered course, remember that:

— All students in a course must have Internet and WWW access to ensure equal opportunities for computer interaction and feedback.

— Students may face the concurrent challenges of learning basic computer skills, new software, and appropriate online communication skills. Trouble-shooting student computer problems will probably become a part of normal instructional responsibilities. Setting up a specific classroom conference for ongoing discussions of specific hardware and software problems may help students to work through these problems on their own.

— Some students might hesitate to contribute to computer conferences or to send e-mail because of a lack of familiarity with the proper protocols.

Encourage students to use e-mail, classroom conferences, electronic bulletin boards, and the WWW early in the course so they overcome inhibitions.

— Using e-mail can help the instructor provide feedback more quickly than surface mail or telephone. Prompt response generally increases student motivation and performance.

— Prompt responses might not always be appropriate. Computer conferences can foster student-to-student interaction. To ensure that this interaction is sustained, work towards a facilitative role. It might be appropriate to delay response to a query in a classroom conference in order to allow students to respond to the issue and to each other.

— Becoming familiar with the resources available on the Internet and the most effective ways to use them will be part of the instructional challenge.

Print Media

Print media is the foundation of distance education and the basis from which all other delivery systems have evolved. The first distance-delivered courses were offered by correspondence study, with print materials sent and returned to students by mail. While technological developments have added to the repertoire of tools available to the distance educator, print continues to be a significant component of all distance education programs.

Various print formats are available, including:

1) *Textbooks.* As in traditionally delivered courses, textbooks are the basis and primary source of content

for the majority of distance-delivered courses. While textbooks should always be critically reviewed before adoption, this is especially critical when the learner and the instructor are not in daily contact.

2) *Study guides.* Typically, distance educators use study guides to reinforce points made during class and through the use of other delivery systems. They will often include exercises, related readings and additional resources available to the student.

3) *Workbooks.* In a distance education context workbooks are often used to provide course content in an interactive manner. A typical format might contain an overview, the content to be covered, one or more exercises or case studies to elaborate the points being made, and a quiz or test for self-assessment. In addition, there is typically some form of feedback, remediation, or "branching" loop to recycle students through the instruction as needed.

4) *Course syllabus.* A comprehensive and well-planned course syllabus is the foundation of many distance-delivered courses. It provides course goals and objectives, performance expectations, descriptions of assignments, related readings, grading criteria, and a day-by-day overview of the material to be covered. The syllabus must be as complete as possible in order to guide the students through the course in the absence of daily contact with the instructor.

5) *Case studies.* If written imaginatively, case studies are an extremely effective instructional tool. In fact, case studies are often designed around the limitations of print and intended to spark the students' imaginations as they place themselves in the particular case under consideration. Many case

studies present a content-based scenario. They raise questions, pose alternative solutions, and then branch students to different sections of the text. There, the consequences of the selected alternative are described.

Because print is largely a one-way communication medium, the challenge is to design instruction to maximize the amount of interaction in distance education print materials. Consider:

Distance educators write instructional materials with language more like that used for speaking than for writing journal articles or books. Some tips for writing instructional materials include:

— Use short sentences.

— Avoid compound sentences.

— Avoid excess information in a sentence.

— Use the active voice.

— Use personal pronouns.

— Keep equivalent items parallel.

— List conditions separately.

— Avoid multiple negatives.

— Use point form.

— Use familiar examples.

— Write as you would speak.

— Avoid unnecessary and difficult words.

— Avoid jargon; use technical terms only when necessary.

— Put sentences and paragraphs into a logical sequence: first things that affect many, then things that affect few; first the general, then the specific; first permanent provisions, then temporary ones.

— Avoid cultural and gender stereotyping.

Advantages

— *Spontaneous.* Print materials can be used in any setting without the need for sophisticated presentation equipment.

— *Instructionally transparent.* The medium of delivery should enhance, not compete with, the content for the learner's attention. If the student reads well, the print medium is the most transparent instructional medium of all.

— *Non-threatening.* Reading is second nature to most students. As a result, they are easily able to focus on the content, without becoming mesmerized or frustrated by the process of reading itself.

— *Easy to use.* Given adequate light, print materials can be used any time and any place without the aid of supplemental resources such as electricity, viewing screen, and specially designed electronic classrooms. The portability of print is especially important for rural learners with limited access to advanced technology.

— *Easily reviewed and referenced.* Print materials are typically learner-controlled. As a result, the student rapidly moves through redundant sections, while focusing on areas demanding additional attention.

— *Cost-effective.* No instructional tool is less expensive to produce than print.

— *Easily edited and revised.* In comparison to technically sophisticated electronic software, print is both easy and inexpensive to edit and revise.

— *Time-effective.* When instructional print materials are created, the developer's primary focus remains on content concerns, not the technical requirements of the delivery system.

Disadvatages

— *Limited view of reality.* Print, by its reliance on the written word, offers a vicarious view of reality. Despite the use of excellent sequential illustrations or photos, for example, it is impossible to adequately recreate motion in print.

— *Passive and self-directed.* Numerous studies have shown that higher learner motivation is required to successfully complete print-based courses. To a certain extent, the passive nature of print can be offset by systematic instructional design that seeks to stimulate the passive learner. Still, it takes more motivation to read a book or work through a written exercise than it does to watch a television program or participate in an audioconference with an instructor encouraging student participation and response.

— *Feedback and interaction.* Without feedback and interaction, instruction suffers, regardless of the delivery system in use. By nature, print materials are passive and self-directed. Even with print materials incorporating feedback mechanisms and interactive exercises, it is easy for learners to skip to the answer section.

— *Dependent on reading skills.* Thanks to television, most students have developed fairly good viewing skills by age four. These same children, however, often fail to develop adequate reading skills by age 12. Reading skills must often be improved. Lack of ability in this area cripples the effectiveness of even the most instructionally sound print material and must be overcome if print is to be used effectively.

Multimedia

Educational use of multimedia has been increasingly strained by its many technologies and this has created an ongoing problem. Integrating multimedia into lesson and unit plans has often meant selecting one or more different machines to play or to enable a communication form.

Once instructors went beyond large charts, globes and pull-down maps, multimedia became much more costly, cumbersome, complicated and less reliable as machines were needed. Further, as many of these machines were expensive, they were not routinely placed in every classroom. Instead, someone needed to make a trip to a media center to obtain the machine, then set it up and adjust it, then return it when finished. An educator might need one cart in the room for the VCR, one for the overhead, one for the record player, another for the stereo system with speakers and radio tuner, and another for the videodisc player and so forth.

If a teacher wanted to create any of these media, even more and different expensive machinery was needed. This situation seriously taxes the time resources of a teacher and the financial resources of a school. From one perspective, this has been further complicated by the advent of personal computers which needed even more expensive projection systems for whole class use and were even more complicated and temperamental in situations where they had to be set up, sometimes connected to other multimedia devices and then returned. On top of all these options, something newer emerged, the multimedia Internet.

Accepting that the old audio-visual agenda such as television and still images on overheads, though somewhat taxing, is still useful to teachers, why is computer-based Internet-delivered multimedia important? First of all, this new development transforms the current situation.

One machine can 'play' each of these media, with the computer acting as media 'jukebox' to a district and Internet storage system of staggering capacity. Further, the same machine with different software applications can be used for the composition of all of these multimedia forms. This is a powerful new development.

Internet capable computers now provide the most cost-effective way to deliver or utilize an enormous and still rapidly growing base of free multimedia based material of great value to educational classroom activity. This includes all eight of the major multimedia forms: text, computer programming, still images, animation, video, audio, virtual reality and device controllers . That is, this includes the software files of multimedia editors such as Powerpoint, Hyperstudio, Premiere and virtual reality applications and more. Further, the Internet provides accessibility to the sound and video samples of a wide array of multimedia that are available for purchase which would never otherwise even be seen for consideration by the average classroom teacher.

In curriculum, significant power belongs to those who can create it and extends to the degree that they do create it. Multimedia technologies today include the most powerful communication form in Western culture, notably motion pictures and their related composition tools. Camcorders are readily available to students and teachers.

Digital video editors allow anyone to easily edit and assemble their own video. Some computer manufacturers are including video editors as a part of the basic application software sold with the computer. With these resources teachers can and will develop and maintain the rights to their own copyrighted video work. Web servers allow the teacher's classroom computer unprecedented power to share videoclip and other media knowledge over greater geographic range than an earth based satellite.

Within seconds of activating the built-in web server of Macintosh and Windows operating systems, or downloading web server freeware from the Internet, any current Internet-capable computer workstation rivals the technical power and global reach of international magazine publishers, and radio and television broadcast stations. This is unprecedented educational power. It is worth re-emphasizing, that beyond becoming effective users of the multimedia based works of others, and international publishers of the work of students, educators can also become creators and composers.

Through multimedia technologies educators can develop work tailored not to the commercial needs of Hollywood, but to the specific educational needs of the students in their classroom.

Computer technology provides a curb-cut that simplifies and accelerates the development of localized multimedia-based curriculum. Further, without this composition knowledge, educators are unable to make the most of Federal "fair use" provisions of the copyright law for multimedia that allow educators to clip and snip images, videoclips and audioclips out of longer works for educational use.

That is, multimedia provides ever greater cultural relevance. For the reason of cultural relevance if no other, educators also need to teach the creation of video and its other multimedia extensions as effectively as they teach the creation of writing. For reasons of professional practice, every teacher needs to become as comfortable composing video as they are composing text. Through such composition, new and popular avenues for imagination, creativity and fantasy emerge.

Every educator depends on some form of multimedia every day. When engaged in higher order skills such as comparison, analysis, inference and evaluation, the mind must carry out its problem processing in some symbol system. Academic skills with verbal language and math are but two important languages (media) for thought.

Though interpersonal and intrapersonal intelligences are not relevant to multimedia use, other intelligences or languages of thought from Gardner's theory are: spatial, bodily kinesthetic, musical, and naturalist. Multimedia development supports and integrates well with this latter set of abilities. That is, multimedia not only extends cognitive range but often takes the thinker to new areas within which to range. Many sequences have been developed to provide a kind of scaffolding for the mind as its works through problems. Further, the different tools sets available for multimedia require sequences which are sometimes complex and relatively lengthy.

Computer-based multimedia enables more complex thinking because of the cognitive based support such software routinely provides. Problems can also be seen as difficulties with a certain perspective. One of the most common ways to attack a problem is to change the perspective in some qualitative way. Multimedia capable teachers have a valuable means for enabling those changes. As composers of multimedia resources, teachers use change of perspective to meet the varied learning styles of different learners.

Educational curriculum appears to have lost sight.of the emphasis on multimedia in culture. It is the classroom that is the back of the pack anomaly. In reference to personal computer technology, multimedia capacity of some sort is generally an assumed feature of computers reaching the market beginning with 1997. Multimedia capacity has been a standard feature of Macintosh computers since 1984.

Even more striking, multimedia forms of information have been the principal means of communication among a significant portion the world's population, with more news and information transferring between phone, radio, television and images than the written word, for a number of years. Television in turn has dominated these other multimedia forms and the written word in terms of the number of hours school-aged children choose a particular medium. This is not to imply that teachers should promote television over the written word or other forms of communication.

But video is just a prominent example of a powerful multimedia communication tool that teachers have historically not been empowered to compose with for their own purposes. Instead, teachers should have the capacity to compose with many media for educational needs as they see fit as they should with any medium that is heavily used by students. Funding sources must continue to expand the portion of the budget that provides for multimedia hardware, software and training and innovative pedogogy which incorporates it.

Within education there are two classes of users of multimedia that need to be emphasized in weighing its relevance: teacher education programs around the country; and schools within range of student teacher population. The influence of focus here will have broad long term influence on the rest of the educational system.

There is an international organization of teacher educators that use technology, SITE. SITE stands for the Society for Information Technology and Teacher Education. It is made up primarily of university faculty in teacher education programs, but also includes school district media specialists, private schools and interested teachers.

Multimedia is an integral part of the design, research, development and teaching concerns of many programs. To the degree that a college and school district is concerned about best of class and leadership with information technology, multimedia capacity and coursework is simply required. Multimedia capacity has provided a number of tangible and less tangible benefits. To educators who are highly dependent on text as the primary means of communication, it can be hard to accept the very powerful aspects of other media in culture. By its nature, the very use of other media competes with time for enhancing ones skills with the medium of text. Obsession with the medium of print and text however is self defeating. Text is enhanced if one accepts the inherent educational challenge to find ways to so meld all media that other media reinforce the value of text and its many efficiencies. We have accepted the value of this capacity without question with "early" readers, books that consist of primarily images with a touch of text. The goal must be to extend the metaphor of "early" readers to the full range of multimedia.

As culture moves towards greater multicultural and multilingual requirements, so must communication evolve with greater facility with multimedia. With any powerful and creative force, there is also a dark side to its power. Under the guise of new technologies, old problems with sexuality, hate, truthfulness and more re-emerge, a problem which requires continual vigilance.

Perhaps the most disturbing is the use of media to desensitize culture to violence. This occurs through not only the acceptance but the glorification of violence in movies, television and music. This development is further magnified by training children and adolescents to kill in realistic simulations during video arcade games. These games use forms of conditioning and training identical or very similar to those used in police and military training. Though educational research is inconclusive in this regard, it remains an issue deserving further attention.

Through the critique of such "curriculum materials" provided byculture, through political lobbying and more, through an understanding of the psychology by which killing is enabled, educators must work strenuously to defang this significant and dangerous use of new media. As the web acquired the power to share such media forms, the computer gained global publishing power.

As the web merges every prior medium, new-age composers will incorporate the full range of metaphor, variation and awareness in one presentation space, with one machine. The computer has become the universal reader. The computer has also become the universal writer. The web page has become the universal form for communication. But the integration is even tighter than the mere parallel display of text, sound and image on one web page. These elements interact.

Within the same web page, a click on text changes adjacent video display. Video display can change text either called automatically as the video plays or with a click within the video display area. Each form can control the timing and display of the other. It is no more proper to think of this as multimedia than it is to think of writing as multi-speech. There is a new level of integration. It is not too far-fetched to conclude that the web-based medium will dominate all prior medium in the twenty-first century. It is worth pausing to let the import of that thought sink in more deeply.

Though the Internet began as a text-only communication system, in the last few years it has matured as an important multimedia publication medium for all the technologies of human communication. Though still in its infancy this medium already provides even individuals with a broadcast range that surpasses all prior technologies in human history.

In the technology research labs the quality of display is already as high or higher than all prior technologies for all media. Further, the form factor for the display of this media is greater than all prior technologies, from screens in research labs that turn and twist in all the sizes and flexibility of paper to functioning stadium size video walls. New generations of communicators must compose for this new world. In contrast with the integrating nature of this medium, education of learners for the emerging world of web composition is fractured, incomplete and balkanized. This is true from elementary school through university graduate programs.

As members and participants in educational system, we have an obligation to organize and develop the merging of all prior communication skills. An opportunity to develop a school of holistic composition. Though the web term of 'linking' is cognitively the shortest term to express the technical aspects of integrating multimedia, linking is insufficient to express the deeper power that it contains. Others promote the term uni-media as a label for this deep integration, though this term is somewhat ambiguous. The phrase comprehensive composition is another offering as a phrase to replace the reign of the term multimedia and less awkward than the holistic composition phrase.

Comprehensive composition involves the planned integration and design of multiple units or forms of communication. At one level it parallels the mechanical skills required in reading (transposition of of written characters into thought) and writing (transfer of thought into written characters). More importantly, linking is open to and parallels the more advanced reflection and organization required of larger structures such as essays, books, and movies.

Future curriculum for 21st century learners must consist of reading, writing and linking a range of multimedia elements. The cultural importance of this transition parallels the magnitude of change initiated by the move thousands of years ago from oral to written culture. With time, reading and writing gained an aura that is represented by the vast depth and range of the content of today's libraries. With time, a similar development will happen with comprehensive composition.

The most recent generations of computer technology have the capacity to become superb multimedia display systems, played from the massive storage of CD-ROMs such as multimedia encyclopedias or downloaded from the gargantuan and still radically expanding resources of the Internet. But even more valuable, personal computers can have the facility to digitize any media and then to compose, transpose, edit and publish, moving the multimedia material from the computer to slide, videotape, audiotape, CD-ROM disc, floppy disk and more. Comprehensive composition has practical benefits as well. This facility to invent with computer-based multimedia allows you to put multimedia needs in the local context, in the context of the learner, and in the display formats available to them.

Computer-based Internet delivered multimedia is the most cost-effective advertising and distribution system for multimedia that is available. Further, computer technology provides curb-cuts for multimedia that simplify its creation and development.

4

Planning and Monitoring of Audio-based Distance Learning

Broadcast media —radio and television —were the first to be used by distance educators, linking the print-based tradition of correspondence education with that of formal and non-formal educational broadcasting. As the technologies became cheaper and more accessible, audio and video cassettes increasingly took over the role of broadcasting, offering greater flexibility and more opportunities for media integration and student-active learning. Again, as the technology became cheaper, more accessible and more powerful, computers and telecommunications became increasingly important, particularly in the more industrialised parts of the world. And this is a trend that is continuing into the 21st century. Also, audio and video tapes were supplemented by high-quality compact disks (CDs), capable of storing large amounts of multi-media material, and by computer-mediated audio via the World Wide Web.

The audio media can't offer the moving images of television and video. Nor can they provide access to the amount of information, or the opportunities for interaction, available from the combination of computers and telephone networks. But the costs of producing the visual media (television, video, computer-based learning), and of using them, are very much higher. And access to the technology, particularly in developing countries, and.especially among the poor and educationally disadvantaged, is still very limited, and likely to remain so well beyond the year 2000. In contrast, radio programmes and audio cassettes are relatively cheap to produce and distribute. Production facilities are widely available.

Access to reception, reproduction and playback facilities is widespread. Even in the poorest rural and urban areas — where the need for distance and open learning is often greatest — radio sets are common, and cassette players are increasingly available.Audio technology is simple, cheap and widely available. The audio media are attractive and popular. They speak directly to their audience in a personal, powerful and persuasive way. They are also extremely effective in terms of teaching and learning — especially when combined and integrated with print and other learning activities.

Uses of Radio for Distance and Open Learning

Radio has the major advantage that it can reach large numbers of listeners, spread over a large geographical area, more or less simultaneously, and at relatively little cost. Here you may find it useful to think of radio as serving the following five main roles or functions. First the list — and then a brief commentary on each of them. The five main roles for radio are:

— News and information

— Motivation and mobilisation

— Tutorial support

— Resource material

— Direct teaching

News and information: Radio can bring up-to-date news and information to distance and open learning students:

— About opportunities and options available to them

— About their courses, course materials, assignments and exams

— About the experience of fellow students and trainees

— About issues of common interest and concern

And because radio is a public medium, it can also inform a wider audience of potential students of what opportunities are open to them, what the courses involve, and what they have to do to enrol.

Motivation and mobilisation: Because radio relies mainly on the human voice, it is a very personal and direct medium. It can provide encouragement and support to students at times when they need it most:

— When they lack confidence to embark on a course of studies

— When they first start studying and are anxious about whether they can cope

— When they are facing their first assignment or examination

— When they are finding the work difficult and are tempted to give up By providing timely encouragement and support, radio can reduce the drop-out rate and increase the rates of course completion.

Tutorial support: Radio can provide tutorial support, both of a general kind and linked specifically to the courses students are studying. For instance:

— Assistance with study skills — organising time, making notes, preparing assignments, revising for and taking exams;

— Introductions to new areas of study and reviews of topics covered;

— Help with key concepts, difficult ideas and new approaches;

— Additional illustrations, examples and explanations, alternative ways of applying knowledge and developing skills;

— Advice, guidance and feedback on study activities and practical work.

In this way, radio tutors can provide the personal contact with a teacher that many distance and open learning students feel they lack.and very much appreciate. It also gives them a sense of being 'real' students, in direct contact with their teachers and the institution.

Resource material: Radio can offer listening and learning experiences that are not readily available through print or face-to-face contact. For instance:

— It can bring students the voices and views of people with particular experience and expertise.

— It can take students to places and situations that they would not normally be able to visit and experience.

— Radio drama can stimulate and excite the imagination; transport students to real and imagined worlds; expose them to ideas and opinions outside their normal experience; explore difficult and sensitive issues; and challenge conventional ways of thinking. Radio can provide examples and illustrations of the application of knowledge and skills. It can present a range of resource material, which students can analyse and evaluate, and which can serve as a stimulus for reflection, discussion and debate.

Direct teaching: Radio can also be used for direct teaching — as a substitute rather than a support to the use of print or face-to-face contact. All of the roles mentioned above can be combined, to form a rich and varied body of teaching and learning materials.

— This is particularly important when open and distance learners have low levels of literacy, or are finding it difficult to adjust to the demands of using printed texts.

— It is also important when sounds are central to the process of teaching and learning — as in language or music teaching.

— In addition, direct teaching by radio can provide valuable support to conventional teachers. It is particularly useful for subjects in which teachers lack confidence or experience, perhaps because of inadequate training or the introduction of new approaches and subjects into the curriculum

Starting in 1971, the British Open University (OU), in partnership with the BBC, used weekly radio programmes (as well as television) in support of its first four Foundation Courses. The programmes were closely integrated with the printed course materials and were accompanied by specially prepared 'broadcast notes'. The BBC and the OU also ran a weekly radio magazine programme called 'Open Forum', providing news and information for OU students and with an opportunity to share their ideas and experiences as distance learners.

In preparation for the launch of the OU, the BBC (in collaboration with the British National Extension College) ran three 'gateway' courses ('Reading to Learn', 'Man in Society' and 'Square Two'), using radio and printed materials, preparing for foundation courses in arts, social sciences and mathematics. These offered potential OU students an opportunity to get back to study and to experience what it was like to be a distance learner.

These were followed in the mid-1970s by two further radio-based distance education courses 'Living Decisions' and 'What Right Have you Got?'. The first dealt with decision-making in the family and the community; the second looked at the rights and responsibilities of the citizen in Britain. Each series consisted of 26 weekly radio programmes, with an accompanying course book. Listeners were invited to join study groups set up by local adult education organisations to follow the series. And for those who wanted a formal qualification, an optional GCE 'O' level exam was available from one of Britain's public examinations boards.

Since the 1980s, radio has been used as the main medium of communication for a series of projects designed to improve the quality of teaching in schools, particularly where there is a shortage of skilled teachers and other learning resources. The project was initiated in the US by the Radio Learning Group, with support from international donors. It was used first for the teaching of mathematics in Nicaragua; later for the teaching of English to Grades 1-3 in Kenya; and was subsequently extended to a number of other subjects in a wide range of developing countries.

The approach involves the intensive use of radio for direct teaching. The programmes are:

— usually 20-30 minutes in length

— broadcast regularly, often daily, throughout the school year

— developed and produced using clear principles of instructional design

— highly interactive, involving frequent student activities in response to the programme material

— supported by specially prepared printed materials for the students

— plus detailed notes for the teachers — on how to prepare the class for listening, what to do during the broadcast, and how the programme material could most effectively be followed up.

IRI pilot projects were carefully monitored and evaluated. Students generally liked using radio and showed significant learning gains. Some teachers were initially sceptical, but grew to value the programmes. However, such programmes were expensive to develop and produce. As a result, although the pilots were generally very successful, in a number of cases governments were unable or unwilling to continue the projects beyond the internationally funded pilot phase.

So far, we've concentrated on the positive side of radio — on its strengths and the unique opportunities it offers to distance and open learners. But what about its drawbacks and disadvantages? What do you see as the main limitations on the effectiveness of radio as a means of communication in distance education and open learning? Here's a list of some of the main disadvantages of the medium. You may want to add others:

— Radio programmes are broadcast at fixed times. These may not always be convenient for students. Also, they may not fit in with the student's work on the other media being used in a course.

— Radio reception in some areas may be poor. Some students will not always be able to receive a clear signal.

— Radio is transitory and ephemeral. Its programmes can usually only be heard once and then they disappear. You can of course record the programmes off-air for later listening: but then we're not really talking about radio, but rather audio cassettes. Also, programmes can be repeated: but that reduces the time available for other educational output.

— The pace of radio is dictated by the broadcasters. Students can't pause to think about what they've just heard. They can't stop the programme to apply knowledge or practise skills.

— Radio is essentially a one-way medium. It talks to the student; but it doesn't usually give the student a chance to answer back — to raise questions or ask for further explanation.

— Radio transmission time is likely to be limited. Teachers and students may not have as much access to the medium as they need. — Also, much of the airtime made available to education tends to be at unsociable and inconvenient hours — late at night or early in the morning And as more radio stations are being privatised, educational broadcasting is becoming much more expensive.

— And of course, radio is a sound-only medium. It lacks the visual dimension that will be very important in many types of teaching and learning..Can you suggest how some of these problems can be overcome? What can be done to maximise the effectiveness of radio and minimise its drawbacks?

To some extent, we can overcome these limitations through good planning and design. We can choose to use radio for appropriate audiences, and for purposes to which it is well suited. We can design radio programmes in such a way that it's easy to learn from them. And we can provide printed materials — specially prepared radio notes — to support the programmes.

Since the 1970s, distance educators have increasingly responded to the limitations of radio by shifting their attention to the production and use of audio cassettes.

Audio cassettes

Audio cassettes have most of the capabilities of radio. They're probably not as good as radio for news and information; but they can certainly fulfil the other four roles — motivation and mobilisation, tutorial support, resource material and direct teaching — as well or better. However, audio cassettes also have a number of added advantages.

— Audio cassettes offer students a much higher level of control over the way they use the material. Provided they have access, either individually or in groups, to cassette players and sources of power, students can listen when, where, how and as often as they like.

— The technology also allows students to stop, start, re-wind and fast- forward the tape. This makes it much easier to integrate the use of audio with other learning materials (e.g. printed texts), and learning activities (e.g. reading, writing, applying what they've learned, practising skills, sharing and discussing ideas and experience).

— Audio cassettes are also generally no more expensive to produce and distribute than radio, unless very large numbers of students are involved. Initial production costs for radio and audio cassettes are likely to be more or less the same. Multi-copying, packaging and distribution of cassettes will involve additional expense; but these costs are generally offset by the fact that radio stations are increasingly tending to charge educational institutions for the transmission of radio programmes. But even if audio cassettes do cost more, this is usually more than justified by their increased educational effectiveness.

Radio still has a role to play, especially in communicating fairly simple messages to large numbers. It is still important in most countries as a source of news and information. Radio is also likely to be important for mass education campaigns and for courses with very large student enrolments. But for most other purposes, the advantages of audio cassettes, even if they involve additional costs, are likely to be overwhelming.

From the 1980s on, the British OU increasingly switched from the use of radio to audio cassettes. This was partly because, as the number of its courses grew, it became more difficult to secure adequate transmission time, and in any case it was difficult to justify using radio for the smaller numbers of students taking each of the more advanced and specialised courses. In addition, however, there was a growing awareness of the educational effectiveness of audio cassettes, particularly in combination with printed and other visual material — what came to be known as 'audio-vision'.

Audio-vision

By audio-vision, we simply mean the combination of audio media — radio and particularly audio cassettes — with visual material. The visual materials are usually in printed form — e.g. specially prepared notes, worksheets, flip-chart illustrations, posters, etc. But they can also be in the form of slides, film strips, models or real objects, either specially provided for the student, or available in the local environment. An example from the British Open University A geology course from the British OU illustrates the range of visual materials that can be used with audio cassettes. In addition to the printed course materials and audio.cassette, students are provided with:

- A film strip with illustrations of different types of rock
- A simple (and cheap) film strip viewer
- A small sample of rock
- A small plastic magnifying glass

The tutor talks to the individual students on the cassette. From time to time, he asks them to look at an illustration in their printed material, or to view a particular frame on the film strip. At one point, the students are asked to inspect a particular surface of the rock sample with the magnifying glass and say what they can see. Then, as they continue to look at the rock sample, the tutor talks them through its distinctive characteristics.

From the teacher's point of view, the combination of audio and visual materials offers at least three major advantages:

— First, it extends the scope and increases the effectiveness of audio. More subjects can be taught more effectively using audio with visual support.

— Secondly, audio-vision promotes student-active learning. This can happen both when the tape is running and when it's been stopped. As well as listening, students are encouraged to look at illustrations, analyse and interpret visual material, and undertake a range of other activities which reinforce learning.

— Third, visual materials also help students concentrate on the audio. Many students find it difficult to concentrate on sound-only material, particularly if they're new to studying with audio. Well designed visuals help students focus their attention on the sounds, and help them get more out of the experience of listening. These three advantages can also be seen as benefits from the students' point of view. Audio-vision means students can be offered audio- based learning on a wider range of subject matter. It encourages greater interaction with the audio materials, with opportunities to apply what they're learning, develop and practise skills, explore attitudes and values, and learn more effectively. Audio-vision also helps them focus on what they're listening to and get more out of it. Students also find that the visual material is often useful as a summary of the audio and an aid to revision. And perhaps most important, most students seem to enjoy using audio-vision. It adds variety and interest to their experience of learning at a distance.

Students Use of Audio Materials in Learning

There are two main factors which affect the way students use audio material in distance and open learning:

— First, there is the way the material is distributed to the students — either through radio broadcasting or in the form of audio cassettes.

— Secondly, there is the question of how the material is intended to be used — either by individual students working on their own or by groups of students working together.

Students listen to radio programmes individually — usually at home. This has the advantage that large numbers of students can be reached simultaneously and at relatively low cost. It also exploits the personal quality of audio — giving the student a sense of having their own individual tutor at home.

Radio programmes also raise the public profile of an institution or project. More people know about the courses and the opportunities they offer if they hear the programmes on the radio. However, this way of using radio also has some disadvantages:

— Students need to have individual access to radio sets and sources of power.

— Good quality radio signals may not reach all areas; reception may be poor.

— Transmission times may not be suitable or convenient for all students.

— Students have little control over how they use a broadcast medium.

— Students listening to radio individually do not usually have the opportunity to follow up what they have heard with other students.

Students listen to radio programmes in groups — usually in local study centres equipped with radio receivers — and often with support and supervision from local tutors or facilitators. Radio still suffers from some of the disadvantages listed above — e.g. poor reception, unsuitable transmission times, a low level of student control. However, provided the study centres are within easy reach of students, they can help to overcome some of the problems of individual access to radio sets.

In addition, group-based listening also offers students the major advantage of being able to discuss what they have just heard and share their reactions with fellow students and often with tutors. It also allows students to participate in a range of group-based follow-up activities — applying knowledge, practising skills, exploring attitudes and values. These activities are an important part of learning, which are not generally available to the individual student listener at home.

Use of audio cassettes

Audio cassettes — particularly in combination with visual materials — offer a powerful educational technology to distance learners. They overcome most of the limitations of radio. Students can use cassettes when, where and as often as they like. They also have a high level of control over how they use the material. They can stop, start and re-wind the tape as they wish; and this also allows a closer integration of audio and print than is possible with radio. However, there are two major limitations to the individual use of audio cassettes:

— First, for courses with large student enrolments, the costs of producing individual cassettes for each student can be substantial.

— Secondly, for students to use cassettes individually, they need individual access to cassette players and sources of power, which may not always be possible.

As with the individual use of radio, students using audio cassettes individually do not normally have the opportunity to share their experience of listening with other students; nor are they able to participate in group-based learning activities which can add substantially to the educational impact and effectiveness of audio and audio-visual materials.

Using audio cassettes in a group context overcomes the main limitations of individual use suggested above:

— Fewer cassettes need to be produced, so production costs are less. — Students do not need personal access to cassette players and power sources.

— Students gain the benefits of audio-based group learning suggested above.

However, the possibility of this type of audio use rests on two important assumptions:

— That the institution or project is in a position to set up and support a network of local study centres which are within a reasonable distance for most of its students;

— That the institution or project is willing and able to equip these centres with audio cassette players suitable for group listening and (if necessary) stand-by sources of power, together with regular servicing and maintenance.

It is also possible to combine these different types of audio use. For instance, an institution could produce radio programmes or audio cassettes for individual use; but also provide alternative listening facilities in local study centres for students who do not have individual access to radio sets or cassette players. It would also be possible for tutors to use radio programmes or audio cassettes aimed primarily at individual students, as a resource for group-based tutorial work at the local centres, for students who want to take advantage of the service.

Choice of audio materials

The choice between these different patterns of audio use depends on a number of inter-related factors. Among the more important, we can identify the following:

— The material and human resources available to an institution or project and the extent to which it is willing to allocate them to audio

— The availability, extent and cost of radio transmission slots

— The extent and quality of radio coverage

— The suitability for students of the available transmission times

— Individual student access to radio sets, audio cassette players and sources of power

— The extent to which an institution or project can set up, support and equip a network of local study centres

— The accessibility and attractiveness of these study centres to students

— The extent of collaboration with other institutions and agencies in providing tutorial support

— The subject matter of the courses being offered and the learning needs of the students

— The numbers and distribution of students following a particular course.

Radio still has a role to play, especially in communicating fairly simple messages to large numbers. It is still important in most countries as a source of news and information. Radio is also likely to be important for mass education campaigns and for courses with very large student enrolments. But for most other purposes, the advantages of audio cassettes, even if they involve additional costs, are likely to be overwhelming. The problem of costs can be addressed by exploring the possibilities of the group-based use of audio cassette technology.

Requirements effective use of audio

Whichever pattern of audio use is adopted for particular courses, the general aim will be to maximise the effectiveness of audio for teaching and learning at a distance. To maximise the effective use of audio, two conditions need to be fulfilled:

— The audio material itself needs to be of high quality. It needs to be carefully planned, designed and developed to meet the needs of the students. It also needs to be skilfully and professionally produced.

— In addition, the audio material needs to be supported by an organisation and managerial system which enables the students to use the material effectively and to derive the maximum educational benefit from it.

Unless students know about the availability of audio material, they will not be in a position to listen to it. The more they know about its purposes and how to use it, the more they are likely to learn from it.

To derive maximum benefit from audio, students need to know the following:

— What audio material is available to them — on radio and/or cassette

— When they can or should listen to the material — radio transmission schedules or suggestions about the best time to use audio cassette material and audio-vision packages

— Why they should listen to audio material — in terms of its aims and objectives, its relationship to other media and learning activities (e.g. printed texts, face-to-face tutorials, assignments and examinations), and its particular contribution to the teaching and learning process

— How they should listen — so that they derive the maximum benefit from the material — how they should prepare for listening, how they can actively engage with the material and how they can reinforce their learning through follow-up activities

For formal courses, there are usually two main options for providing information about audio to students.

First, information on audio can be included in the main printed text(s) for the course. This has the advantage of presenting audio and printed materials in a fully integrated way. However, this approach can present the production team with practical problems. Even in the best planned courses, the schedules for the development and production of audio tend to lag behind those for printed texts. As a result, all the information students need about audio may not be available at the time the text has to be delivered to the printer..

If subject specialists are under pressure to produce new courses, what often happens is that they concentrate their efforts on the preparation of printed materials; and courses are launched initially without audio support, which is then added later. Also, if the course is using radio, transmission schedules tend to vary from year to year; and it is therefore not possible to include accurate and up-to-date information about when programmes will be broadcast in the main course text(s), which would normally be used over a number of years.

Secondly, as an alternative to including audio information in the main course text(s) — for instance, in the examples cited above — the information can be presented in specially prepared and separately bound audio notes. The main course text(s) will usually contain brief references to audio; but the detailed information about the audio material and how to use it will be presented in the separately published audio notes.

In both cases, there is also a strong case for repeating and reinforcing essential information (aims, objectives, how to use the materials, follow-up activities) in the audio material itself. If students receive the information from at least two sources, there is a better chance that it will get through to them and be absorbed.

The two options outlined above — plus the inclusion of information in the audio materials themselves — can also be used with audio for non-formal education. However, many non-formal courses will be aimed at audiences with a significant proportion of non-literate or semi-literate listeners and learners. In these cases, the use of printed information alone will have limited impact. In this situation, distance educators need to look to other ways of communicating with the target audience. Here, general programmes on radio and television can play an important role in reaching the target audience. They can provide information on what is available, when and where it can be heard, and how to enrol in non-formal education courses.

However, announcements in the mass media are unlikely in themselves to motivate and mobilise the potential audience into active participation in non-formal education. These messages need to be supported and reinforced by credible local sources of information and advice.

For this reason, in addition to promoting and publicising non-formal courses through the mass media, you also need to gain access to a range of local communication networks, which can support and endorse the mass media messages. In the formal sector, such support is often available through a network of local study centres. However, these centres tend to be fully occupied with the support of formal.courses and are unlikely to have the resources to extend their activities to the non-formal sector. So for non-formal courses, you usually have to seek out and work through alternative networks to reach and support students.

It is important to distinguish between the provision of information for formal and non-formal courses.

Providing information on audio for students who are registered for formal courses should not create too many difficulties. You are usually in direct and regular contact with these students. The audio material is usually a component of a print-led multi-media package. Information on audio can therefore be included in the main course texts which are distributed to students — usually by post or via local study centres — or in separate Audio Notes which can be distributed with the main texts and other course materials.

Even in this case, however, there can be problems. These are likely to relate mainly to scheduling — e.g. coordinating the schedules for the development and production of audio and printed materials, so that information about the audio component is available when it is required for presentation in print. In addition, as with any distance education materials, there can also be problems in situations where the physical distribution of materials to remote areas presents difficulties.

Much greater problems tend to arise in the communication of information about non-formal courses — for instance, where radio is being used as the main medium in a mass education campaign. In this case, you are unlikely to have the same sort of direct contact with potential students that is available for formal courses. Instead, you will need to explore and establish alternative channels of communication; and this in turn will involve research, dialogue, liaison, cooperation and collaboration with a wide range of other institutions and agencies that are in a position to offer such alternative communication systems.

The specific institutions and agencies will depend on the particular audiences at which the non-formal programmes are aimed. For instance:

— A radio-based course designed to improve agricultural practices might seek to communicate with potential students (i.e. farmers) through a national or regional network of agricultural extension workers.

— A non-formal health promotion course or campaign might seek to disseminate information through local health workers and clinics. It might also involve national or regional women's organisations.

In both these cases and others, you might also seek to promote the courses and involve potential students through a number of other networks. For instance, the networks of local personnel offered by the formal education system (schools, colleges, universities); by the structures of national and local government; or through a range of well-established and respected NGOs and other voluntary agencies with a particular interest or involvement in non-formal education. The challenge that presents itself to those involved in using audio for non-formal distance and open learning is therefore:

- To identify appropriate networks through which to contact and communicate with specific target audiences for non-formal education
- To establish and develop close working relationships, characterised by mutual trust and respect, with the institutions and agencies that have access to and control over these communication networks
- To design and deliver persuasive messages that will inform, motivate and mobilise potential students to involve themselves actively in non-formal audio-based courses

Responding to this challenge requires a substantial investment in planning and research, and in establishing and maintaining successful collaborative partnerships. This activity inevitably takes time and money. One of the key questions, therefore, is what proportion of the audio budget should be invested in promotion and publicity for non- formal courses.

Resources and facilities

In the case of individual listening to audio materials, it is usually assumed that students will have individual access to their own radio receivers and/or audio cassette players; and that they will also have regular access to adequate sources of power. However, it is also widely recognised, particularly in poorer countries, that such access to audio equipment and facilities cannot always be guaranteed. This raises important questions of equity for those involved in distance and open learning. If some students have access to audio, while others don't, does this give the students who have access an unfair advantage over those who do not? A common response to this problem is to make audio an 'optional extra' in courses, rather than an integral component of the teaching and learning package. As a result, the status of audio is down-graded. It tends to be seen as a non-essential part of the course. As a result, the full potential of the medium is rarely achieved and exploited.

For these reasons, many distance and open learning institutions provide radio and audio cassette listening facilities in their local resource and study centres. In this way, students who do not have individual access to audio equipment and/or sources of power can come into their local study centre, provided it is within a reasonable distance of where they live, and listen to the audio materials for their courses. If it is reasonable to assume that all students will be able to listen either at home or in a study centre, then the status of audio can be up-graded, it can be defined as an essential part of the teaching and.learning system, and there is a better chance that the full potential of the medium will be realised.

In addition, once local resource and study centres have been equipped with audio listening equipment, it also becomes possible to start producing audio material, both radio and especially cassettes, designed specifically for group listening. This also makes it possible to offer students a wide range of audio-based group learning activities:

— Applying knowledge in the local environment

— Developing and using practical skills

— Discussing and evaluating attitudes and opinions

— Sharing experience and learning from each other

Group-based use of audio, especially in combination with print, can also provide tutors with additional resource material, make tutorial sessions more varied and interesting, and generally add to the attractiveness and satisfactions of learning at a distance. Providing facilities such as those suggested above makes significant demands in terms of human and material resources. In effect, the system would require:

— Equipping each study centre with at least one radio-audio cassette players, with sufficiently powerful speakers to use them in group situations of up to say 20 students, and also with headphones for individual listening.

— Providing the centres with either stand-by generators or sufficient supplies of dry-cell batteries to enable the equipment to be used when mains electricity is not available; in this connection it might also be worth investigating the comparative costs of using solar power or of investing in the recently developed clockwork radios, due to be followed by a clockwork cassette player.

— It would also be necessary to set up a system for the servicing, maintenance and repair of the equipment — with spare radio- cassette players to cover periods when equipment was out of action.

— Study centres would also need to be supplied with a complete set of audio cassette and audio-visual materials; and these would need to be catalogued for easy access by students and tutors.

— Once these resources and facilities are in place, it would also be necessary to appoint someone to take responsibility for their management and control, and also to provide a means of storing them securely — e.g. a locked steel cupboard.

Support for audio use

The effective use of audio will be increased if students are provided with support and guidance on how to use the materials. This support and guidance can be provided in three main ways:

— In printed form — either in the course text(s), or in specially prepared Audio Notes.

— Through the provision of specially trained tutors or study group leaders or facilitators

— By a combination of both methods — print plus tutorial or facilitator support

Printed support: Printed information and tutorial support for students using audio — particularly for individual use in formal education — is usually provided, either in the main course text(s), or in specially prepared Audio Notes. In whatever form the information is presented, it usually contains the following main elements:

— A statement of the aims and objectives of the audio material and its accompanying print — what the student can expect to learn from listening to the material and doing the associated activities

— A brief introduction to the main content and structure of the material — what subjects are covered, in what order, who is taking part, what they have to offer, plus any background information which is relevant to what the students will hear

— Suggestions on how to prepare for listening — sections of the course text that should have been completed, knowledge and skills assumed, and (in the case of audio cassettes) an indication of when it would be most useful to listen

— Any visual material to be used in conjunction with the audio — e.g. charts, diagrams, tables, maps, illustrations etc. which the students will need look at while listening — plus (in the case of cassettes) any activities or exercises to be done when the tape is stopped

— Details of any follow-up activities to be completed after listening to the audio material — plus (where appropriate) self-check answers to exercises undertaken during the programme, a glossary of new words and key concepts and suggestions for further reading and study activities.

Similar support material is often provided for audio material that is mainly intended for group listening. This is particularly the case in formal distance education programmes; but such materials are also sometimes produced for non-formal courses. However, when audio is produced mainly for group listening, whether in formal or non-formal education, in addition to providing printed support materials, it is also usual to provide face-to-face tutorial support or study group leadership designed to facilitate the group-based use of the audio material.

Personal support: The provision of face-to-face tutors and study group leaders or facilitators in support of audio involves three main activities — recruitment, training and providing support and supervision.

1) *Recruitment*: In most formal distance education systems it is not usually necessary to recruit tutors to work specifically on audio. Normally, local part-time tutors will have been recruited to provide general tutorial support for students, which will include work with audio materials. However, it is important to take account of the role of audio in recruiting part-time tutorial staff — for instance:

— In defining the tutors' role and responsibilities, and preparing job descriptions

— In negotiating terms and conditions of employment and drafting contracts

— In selection procedures and in initial briefing and induction programmes

In non-formal education, you are more likely to be recruiting local part-time tutors or study group leaders to work specifically with audio-based learning groups. As with general face-to-face tutors, it will be necessary:

— To define roles and prepare job descriptions

— To negotiate terms and conditions of employment

— To draft and issue formal contracts of employment

— To devise selection and induction procedures

However, whereas part-time tutors for formal courses will tend to be drawn from conventional education (schools, colleges, universities), non-formal tutors and study group leaders/facilitators will typically come from a much wider range of institutions and agencies. This is an area in which effective collaboration will be very important — with government departments, voluntary organisations (NGOs) and the private sector.

In some areas of non-formal education, you may lack professional experience and expertise. It is also possible that you may not have the grass-roots contacts to be able to recruit suitably qualified and experienced local tutors, trainers and facilitators. Collaboration with government departments, NGOs and the private sector will therefore be essential..For these collaborations to work well, they need to begin early in the course development process. Consultation needs to start at the planning and design stage. Collaboration needs to be continued through the development and production of materials and the setting up and staffing of local study centres. It is also important that partner agencies should be involved in the monitoring and evaluation of projects, their modification and improvement, and the development of new initiatives.

2) *Training:* Once the local part-time tutors and study group leaders have been recruited and introduced to the idea of distance and open learning, they then need to be trained in how to help students derive the maximum benefit from audio and accompanying printed and visual materials. This applies equally to formal and non-formal education. In formal courses, audio training will normally be included as part of a more general package of tutor training. A similar approach may also be adopted for non-formal courses; though here training in the use of audio will often need to play a more prominent part. The specific content of audio training will vary from

course to course. But the general principles underlying the process remain essentially the same.

Identifying training needs — Most of your potential tutors and facilitators will have had relatively little experience of using audio for education and training. Your first task is therefore to identify and analyse their training needs:

— What knowledge, skills and attitudes will their role require?

— What do they know already? What skills do they already have? — What knowledge and skills do they need to acquire? What attitudes and values need to be challenged or reinforced?

Designing training courses, workshops and materials — Once you have identified the training needs of your tutors/facilitators, the next task is to design and develop a programme of training to respond to these needs. This may be delivered independently, or as part of a broader programme of tutor training. The specific content of the training will be determined by the background and experience of the trainees and the specific course for which they are being trained. However, most training programmes will probably include the following main items:

— An introduction to the students, their background and learning needs

— An overview of the course as a whole and its main components

— An introduction to the role of audio and audio-vision in the course

— A review of the aims, objectives and content of the audio and associated print

— How to organise and manage an audio-based tutorial or training session

— How to encourage and support student participation and active learning

— How to monitor, evaluate and improve audio-based teaching and learning

3) *Support and supervision*: Once tutors and facilitators have been trained in the use of audio, it is important to provide them with continuing support and supervision. This will help them develop their skills and improve the quality of service they offer to the students. In addition, there also needs to be a system that ensures the technology necessary for audio (radio-audio cassette players, sources of power and supplies of audio cassettes) is properly serviced and maintained. There are several ways in which a system of support and supervision can be organised. The system adopted will obviously depend to a considerable extent on the size and scope of the institution or project. Here, as an illustration, we look at what might be provided in a fairly large institution operating at local, regional and national levels. Smaller organisations would be likely to have a less elaborate structure; but they would still need to fulfil the same functions.

— *Local mentoring* — At the local level there should be a system of 'mentoring' — i.e. tutors/facilitators with successful experience of using audio should be appointed as 'mentors', to provide informal day-to-day advice, guidance and support to new or less experienced tutors in how they can make the best use of the medium.

— *Regional supervision* — At the regional level, more senior staff should be appointed to take special responsibility for the support and supervision of the use of audio. This would involve, for instance:

— Making regular visits to local tutorial/study groups — to monitor and evaluate the use of audio; to check on equipment, facilities and resources; and to provide advice, guidance and support to tutors on their use of audio.

— Making regular reports and providing feedback on the impact and effectiveness of radio, audio cassettes and audio-vision, and putting forward suggestions on how the quality of audio materials and tutorial service might be improved.

— *Central coordination* — At national level, a senior member of the student support staff should be appointed with special responsibility for:

— Coordinating, analysing and interpreting information and feedback received from the regional staff on the use, impact and effectiveness of radio and audio cassette materials.

— Providing regular reports to subject specialists and producers on the use of radio, audio cassettes and audio-vision, with recommendations on how the materials and services could be improved.

— Providing support and supervision to the regional staff responsible for audio; keeping them informed on developments in relation to audio at the national level; and representing their interests and needs in policy and planning discussions.

Organising and managing the recruitment, training and support of staff with responsibilities for audio makes substantial demands on institutions and projects. In return, however, not only is the impact and effectiveness of audio likely to increase, but (as indicated above) you will also have access to an extensive network of trained tutorial staff, in close and regular contact with your students. These tutors and facilitators will be in an excellent position to provide valuable information and advice on the audio materials you are producing and on how your audio services can be improved.

Audio Planning

There are three levels of audio planning:

— *Institutional planning* — involving the allocation of resources for audio to particular areas of an institution's activities usually expressed in terms of policy, staffing and budgets.

— *Series planning* — which involves the planning and design of a series of radio programmes or audio cassette materials linked to a particular course or programme of studies, usually presented in the form of a fairly general series outline.

— *Programme planning* — which covers the detailed planning and design of individual radio programmes or audio cassette sequences, and is usually put on paper in the form of a detailed programme or audio cassette outline.

Institutional planning involves making decisions about the overall allocation of resources — human, technical, financial — to the planning, development, production and distribution of audio materials. These decisions are usually made at a senior management level within an institution. In relation to audio, the senior management team of a distance or open learning institution typically has to decide:

— What proportion of the budget should be allocated to audio — as opposed, for instance, to the production of printed materials, television or video, the provision of student support services, etc.

— How the audio budget should be distributed between different departments, programmes of study, perhaps even down to the level of individual courses.

— How to make the most efficient and effective use of the professional skills and technical facilities available to the institution.

To make such decisions rationally, planners and managers need good quality advance information, about the range of options available to them, and the extent to which the various options are likely to help the institution achieve its goals — e.g. to provide the best quality distance and open learning to the largest number of educationally disadvantaged students.

For an institution to make rational choices on the allocation of resources to audio, it needs clear advance information on how, why and with what effect, different departments and courses are proposing to use audio. This is exactly the type of information that a carefully prepared series outline provides. Such an outline will typically cover:

— who the audio is intended for

— what contribution it will make to teaching and learning

— what it will cover and what form it will take

— how it will be integrated with other media and learning activities

— what will be involved in developing and producing the materials

— how the audio material is intended to be used by the students

— how its impact and effectiveness will be monitored and evaluated

Armed with this information, planners and managers can make comparisons and rational choices between the different options presented to them; and in this way maximise the efficiency and effectiveness with which an institution uses its scarce resources.

It is worth noting that agreeing on a clear series outline leads to a number of positive advantages for those involved in developing and producing the audio materials. For instance:

— The series outline provides clear guidelines on the amount and type of audio to be produced. It will also spell out the role of audio in relation to other media and learning activities.

— It will also become possible to integrate the development and use of audio more closely with that of other media being used and with the face-to-face support offered to students at tutorial sessions and residential courses.

— This in turn will make it possible to exploit the unique characteristics of different media; to use them in a way that maximises their effectiveness; and to provide the students with better quality learning materials, and a more interesting, satisfying and worthwhile experience of studying at a distance.

In this way, the preparation of series outlines for audio not only makes it possible for institutions to undertake rational forward planning, but also enables subject specialists and media staff to make the most effective use of audio and other media in distance and open learning. This is why series planning is important.

Generally a checklist for audio planning include:

— Audience

— Aims and objectives

— Content and structure

— Form and format

— Support material

— Resources, scheduling, monitoring and evaluation

Audience: In planning any audio series, it's important to know the main characteristics of your target audience. Without this knowledge, it's difficult to know how to communicate with them in a way that they'll understand and respond to. Some key questions:

— What do you need to know about your target audience?

— How much of this information do you have already?

— What do you need to find out?

— How can the information be obtained?

What we're doing here is preparing an 'audience profile'. There are at least three types of information that you'll find useful:

— *Demographic data* — e.g. information on age, gender, literacy and education levels, occupation, environment (e.g. rural/urban), etc..— Knowledge, skills and attitudes — information on what the students are likely to know already, what they can do, their attitudes to the subject matter and their expectations of the course.

— Access, facilities and study skills — access to audio equipment (radios, cassette players, sources of power), quality of reception, experience of learning from audio.

It's easy enough to identify the information you need. It's usually more difficult to obtain it. Some of the information may already be available — from colleagues, from other educational institutions, from national and local organisations.

If the information is available, do your best to obtain it. If not, or if you suspect the information may be inaccurate or out-of-date, you'll need to try and obtain it for yourself. There are a number of ways of doing this — e.g. sample surveys, questionnaires, interviews. But most of these methods are expensive and time- consuming, especially in developing countries. Probably the most efficient and economic way of obtaining the information you need is to meet with a small number of 'focus groups' — i.e. groups of people who are broadly representative of the audience you're aiming at.

The information you obtain may not be statistically representative of the target audience. But it will at least give you a chance to discuss the questions raised above with a group of people who are fairly typical of your potential students, and will help you begin to see the world from their perspective. There's no standard way of presenting an audience profile. You can organise it in whatever way you find most useful. Once you've completed the task, the next step is to start thinking about how the audience profile will influence and shape the way you design and present your audio series.

In general, the audience profile should help you decide:

— What the students want and expect from the course and its audio material

— The prior knowledge, skills and attitudes you can assume from your students

— The level and style of language that will be appropriate

— The type of examples and illustrations you should use

— Whether to use radio or audio cassettes — or neither or both

— Whether to aim for individual or group use of the audio materials

— What type of support material and study activities would be appropriate

Aims and objectives: When planning audio for distance and open learning, it's important to be clear about exactly what you want to achieve through the use of the medium. One way of clarifying your thinking on this is to spell out your general aims and specific objectives in using audio.

Content and structure: Once you've identified and characterised the audience, and defined your aims and objectives, then it's time to go on to the content and structure of the audio series. You've answered the 'who?' and 'why?' questions; now we turn to the questions of 'what?' and 'how?': What content do you want to include in the audio series? How should this content be organised for presentation to the students? If you've defined your aims and objectives clearly, identifying content and deciding on a structure or sequence should not be difficult. In order to achieve each objective, you'll need to present a certain amount of 'content' — i.e. appropriate audio material. And for this content to make sense to the students, it will need to be presented in a logical and coherent order.

Once you have identified the audience, defined your aims and objectives and decided on the main content and structure of your audio series, then you are probably in a position to start preparing a general series outline. This usually includes information on:

— The target audience

— The aims and objectives for audio

— The subject matter to be covered

— The order in which it will be dealt with

— The relationship of audio to other parts of the course — e.g. printand face-to-face contact

There's no standard format for this outline. But you might find it useful to present the information in the following type of table.

Form and format: There are two main types of decision you need to make here:

— First, whether to distribute the audio material to students through broadcasting or in recorded form — i.e. whether to use radio programmes or audio cassettes

— Secondly, what particular forms and formats of audio will enable you to communicate most effectively with your students.

Form and format: Radio has the great advantage of reaching large numbers of students simultaneously and at relatively low cost. But it also has the major disadvantage of giving students relatively little control over their use of the audio.materials. Audio cassettes may involve additional copying and distribution costs, but they offer a much higher level of student control. As a result, audio materials can be more closely integrated with other media and learning activities, and this can make possible more student-active learning.

Your decision on whether to use radio or audio cassettes will usually depend on the following main factors:

— Your target audience — the number of potential students, their geographical spread, and their access to audio technology and sources of power — The type of course and subject matter you're teaching (e.g. formal/non-formal), the role of the audio material and its relationship to other media and learning activities

— Your access to suitable radio transmission times and the competing demands for them from other programmes and courses

— The relative costs of distributing the material on radio and on cassette, and your judgement about the educational benefits of using one medium rather than the other

The second type of decision you need to make, whether you're distributing by radio or on audio cassette, is about how you can use the medium most effectively. This is in part a question about audio forms and formats. By 'form' we mean a particular type of audio material. By 'format' we mean the different ways in which these forms can be combined, to communicate with your students. Detailed decisions about form and format are usually made at a later stage, when individual programmes or audio sequences are being developed. But even at an early stage of planning, it's necessary to think in general terms about the type of audio material you're likely to use, since this will have important implications in terms of the resources you'll need (human, technical, financial) and the time it will take you to develop and produce the audio materials.

Just as ideas for subject matter grow out of your thinking about aims and objectives, so ideas for form and format need to emerge from decisions made about content. Content should dictate form and format; not the other way around.

The range of audio forms is extensive. These forms can either be used on their own — talks, interviews, discussion, drama — or they can be combined into various formats. The range of formats is only limited by the imagination and creativity of the scriptwriters and audio producers. Some of the more common formatsare illustrated below.

— *Documentaries*: Factual reports on past or present questions, issues, situations or events, incorporating narrative, description and analysis, and usually combining several of the following elements — scripted talk, interviews, discussion, actuality and/or archive material.

— *Features*: Audio material dealing with similar factual themes to documentaries, but approaching them in a more imaginative, creative and artistic way, often incorporating elements of music and drama.

— *Magazines*: A popular and widely used format; usually broadcast on a regular basis (daily, weekly, monthly); dealing with a number of different topics, linked by a common theme; using a range of different audio forms; and usually presented (in distance education) by an audio teacher or tutor.

— *Drama with tutorial commentary*: Audio material relying mainly on drama to communicate with students; but including tutorial commentary, usually offering introduction, interpretation and reinforcement of the themes explored in the drama.

There are no rules and regulations that govern the choice of forms and formats. This is essentially a creative and imaginative task.

Support material and activities: The educational impact and effectiveness of audio can be substantially increased by combining audio media with specially prepared visual materials. Combining and integrating audio with visual elements — i.e. creating audio-vision — encourages the active involvement and participation in the process of listening and learning. You may find it useful to think about the combination of audio and visual materials in terms of a 'before- during-after' sequence.

Combining audio and visual materials:

1) Before listening: Visual material can help prepare students for listening.

   — What would it be useful for students to read, look at, think about or investigate, before they start listening to a particular piece of audio?

   — What activities and preparations would help them get the most out of the audio material they'll be listening to?

2) *During listening*: Having something relevant to look at while you are listening helps concentration and promotes active learning. In addition, by combining sound with appropriate visual images, it's possible to extend the range of subject matter that audio can deal with. Audio-vision is a relatively low cost but potentially very powerful educational technology.

   — What would it be useful for students to look at while they are listening? How could visual material enhance or extend the experience of listening and learning?

   — Are there other things that students could usefully do while listening to audio — e.g. examining objects, carrying out tasks, reacting on paper to what they're listening to?

   — In the case of cassettes, are there exercises and activities that students could usefully do when the tape is stopped? How could you use printed/visual materials to offer students opportunities to apply knowledge, practise skills and reflect on attitudes and values, and generally to support and reinforce their learning from audio?

3) *After listening*: Here visual material can be used for a range of follow- up, reinforcement and revision exercises and activities.

   — What would it be useful for students to do after they have listened to a piece of audio material? How can print encourage and support such activities?

   — How can support materials encourage the application of newly acquired knowledge, the practice and development of skills and the further exploration of attitudes and values?

   — How can support materials promote the longer term impact and influence of audio in distance and open learning?

Resources, scheduling, monitoring and evaluation: Although resources, scheduling, and monitoring and evaluation are important aspects of series planning, we'll delay our discussion of them until we've looked more closely at who should be involved in planning, and how it should be organised and managed; and also until we've considered what is involved in the development and production of audio materials. There are at least two key roles that need to be involved in the planning and design of audio for most types of distance and open learning:

— *Subject specialists* — preferably with knowledge and experience, not only of teaching the subject at an appropriate level, but also of the particular audience for whom the audio materials are intended

— *Audio producers* — preferably with professional experience of educational broadcasting and/or audio cassette production in areas close to the subject matter of the course, and again familiar with the target audience

There are also a number of other professional skills that can make a useful contribution to the planning and design of audio and its supporting materials. Among the more important are the following:

— *Educational technologists/instructional designers* — with a particular interest in how adults learn at a distance, and skills in designing adult learning materials

— *Local tutorial staff* — who are familiar with the target audience and can advise on their particular learning needs and the type of study materials that are likely to be most useful to them

— *Print specialists and graphic designers* — who can advise on the design and layout of printed and visual support materials

— *Evaluation specialists* — who can investigate and advise on the impact and effectiveness of audio and printed support materials as they are being developed and when they are being used by students

The contributions of the first two professional roles are fairly self- evident:

— *Subject specialists* — provide knowledge of the subject you want to teach. They normally determine what the content of the audio material will be. So it's important that their knowledge is accurate and up-to-date; and that they also have experience in teaching the subject to the type of target audience you're aiming at.

— *Audio producers* — bring knowledge and skills in how to communicate effectively using sound. They should be able to suggest the subject matter that can best be dealt with through audio; the forms and formats that are available; and how they can be used most effectively. At a later stage, audio producers will also play a key role in realising the ideas that emerge from the planning stage in the form of radio programmes and audio cassettes that the students listen to.

The contributions of the other three professional roles are perhaps less immediately self-evident:

— *Educational technologists/instructional designers* — have expertise in the dynamics of the teaching and learning process. They should therefore be able to advise on the structuring of the audio material, the design of visual support and audio-based learning activities, and the relationship of audio to other components of a course.

— *Local tutors* — will bring to planning and design their knowledge and experience, not only of the students, but also of the environments in which they live and work: the facilities available to them, the particular problems they face and the type of support they need. For this reason, they will be especially useful in advising on whether to use radio or audio cassettes; whether audio should be used individually or in groups; and what type of support material would be most helpful.

— *Print specialists and graphic designers* — will be able to contribute in the design and layout of printed and other visual materials developed in support of audio. They will also have a particular role to play, working closely with educational technologists/instructional designers, in advising on the effective integration of audio materials and the printed components of a course, and later in implementing decisions in this area in the development and production process.

— *Evaluation specialists* — will probably not have a major role in the early stages of planning. But it's important that they should be involved from the start, so that they have a clear idea of what the course is trying to achieve, and the evolving logic of the approach adopted. In this way, they'll be in a better position to advise those involved in developing the audio and support material during the process of formative evaluation.

Two further points need to be made before we move on — which will lead us into our final question:

— First, not all of these professionals need to be involved in all stages of the planning and design process. As we move from institutional.to series and programme planning, the degree and type of involvement of the different roles will change.

— Secondly, in multi-media distance education, those involved in the planning and design of audio (and other media) tend to be a sub- group in a larger course planning and development team, which involves other specialists and probably also needs administrative and managerial support.

These two points raise a number of important questions about the organisation and management of the planning process.

We now turn to the question of how the different professional roles outlined above can be organised and managed to plan and produce effective audio materials for distance and open learning. The question is not an easy one, since the different roles are drawn from very different professional backgrounds.

— Subject specialists — usually come from academic and teaching backgrounds. They often tend to be more concerned with the content of their subject than with the different ways it can be communicated. They may have some experience of communicating through print; but often they have little or no experience of electronic media, including radio and audio cassettes.

— Audio producers — will usually have come from a broadcasting background, and will have professional experience in communicating through electronic media. As a result, their main interest is likely to be in the medium; and they may have little or no knowledge or experience of the academic discipline or subject area on which they are working.

Similarly, educational technologists/instructional designers, local tutorial staff and evaluation specialists will all approach planning from a particular professional perspective. In addition, the different backgrounds may also raise questions of relative status and seniority.

Moulding this type of diverse group into a coherent planning team may not be easy. What kind of problems are likely to arise within multi- disciplinary planning teams? What particular problems might arise between subject specialists and media personnel? How do you think these problems might be resolved?

In fact, it's fairly common in distance and open learning institutions for there to be some degree of conflict and tension between subject specialists and media staff. Subject specialists sometimes regard media producers as focusing too much on the process of 'communication' and not being sufficiently concerned with content. They see them as being more concerned with the 'medium' than with the 'message'.

Media producers tend to see subject specialists as being too narrowly concerned with questions of 'content', and not paying sufficient attention to the way in which the content is communicated. At its worst, this type of tension can lead to conflict between the two groups. And if the conflict is not resolved, it can lead to a breakdown in communication, to the detriment of the learning materials being planned and designed. Often the situation is made more difficult by status differences between subject specialists and media staff within an institution.

Perhaps the best known solution to this type of problem is that developed by the British Open University in the early 1970s, and later adopted and modified by a number of other distance teaching institutions — i.e. that of the 'course team'. Essentially, the approach involves setting up a multi- disciplinary team — including subject specialists, media personnel and other professionals — who meet together on a regular basis, and take collective responsibility for the planning, design and development of a distance education course. The great strength of this approach is that, at its best, it can produce a mutually inter-dependent group of professionals, with a shared ideology, and developed skills in producing high quality and carefully integrated distance and open learning materials. .The main disadvantages of the course team approach are that:

— It tends to be very demanding and expensive in terms of staff time

— It requires a capacity for long term planning which many institutions find difficult to establish

— It involves an open and democratic style of management which for some participants may be unfamiliar and uncomfortable

In practice, relatively few institutions operate a fully developed course team model. In most, the design and development of courses is the responsibility of a relatively small group of people, who may from time to time call on others to assist them. In this context, there is relatively little opportunity to develop a shared professional outlook.

Management tends to be hierarchical; the potential for conflict between different specialists is increased; and the degree of integration between different media tends to be reduced. In this type of situation, the opportunity to realise the full potential of audio is limited. In print-led courses — mainly in formal education — ideas for print are usually developed first, with audio being planned later.

Audio producers are not usually involved in the initial planning; and there's little opportunity to develop the collaborative approach mentioned above. As a result, the potential for conflict between audio producers and subject specialists in the planning and development of audio material is increased. The unique strengths of audio tend not to be exploited. And audio is often grafted on, as a supplementary component, which is peripheral to the main body of the teaching system. For these reasons, there is a strong case for having some sort of course team, with collective responsibility for the planning and design of audio materials, in conjunction with other teaching and learning materials. The essential members of such a team are subject specialists and audio producers.

Monitoring and Evaluation

Research and evaluation involve specialist skills. The more sophisticated the research task, the higher the level of skill and experience required. Most distance and open learning institutions have at least some provision in this area. In most institutions, the number of research and evaluation personnel is likely to be very limited. It is also likely that they will concentrate their efforts on the evaluation of 'products' and on student access and responses to them. This work is obviously important. But it also leaves a large area of 'process' uncovered — particularly the planning, design, development and production processes.

Senior staff — department heads and heads of sections — have a major responsibility in this area; and this needs be written into their job descriptions. In particular, their responsibilities should include:

— Establishing agreed procedures, ways of working and performance standards within their areas of responsibility

— Communicating these norms, values and expectations to the staff involved, and negotiating their acceptability

— Monitoring and evaluating activity within their area of responsibility

— identifying problems, seeking solutions and securing their implementation — in consultation with the staff involved

— Creating an awareness and acceptance of the idea of 'total quality' by all staff, and motivating them to take responsibility for achieving high standards of quality, effectiveness and efficiency

From this it is clear that senior staff on their own cannot carry responsibility for monitoring and evaluating performance and ensuring high standards of quality. Procedures and standards of performance need to be negotiated, agreed and accepted by all staff if high standards are to be achieved. However, senior staff do have a special responsibility for providing leadership and establishing a 'culture of quality' within their areas of responsibility — a set of attitudes and behaviours, permeating the organisation, that reflect a commitment to the values of quality, relevance, effectiveness and efficiency in distance and open learning.

Recognising that monitoring and evaluation of audio is not just the responsibility of a small group of research and evaluation specialists has two major implications:

— The need to set up on-going systems for monitoring and evaluating audio-related activities at all levels within an organisation

— The need to provide training in the techniques of monitoring and evaluation — in particular for management, but also for a wider range of staff involved in the design, development and delivery of audio materials

Methods

A wide range of research methods and techniques are available for the monitoring and evaluation of audio-related activities in distance education. Among the more important are the following:

— *Internal review* — in which colleagues review, discuss and evaluate their own procedures, practices and performance. This can be done formally by setting targets and reviewing progress on a regular basis. Such reviews can be conducted individually or collectively.

— *External assessment* — in which outside experts review specific areas of audio-related activity, and provide evaluative comment and suggestions for improvement — e.g. external assessors and examiners for particular courses, outside consultants advising on the design, development, production and delivery of audio materials.

— *Sample survey methods* — in which questionnaires and interview schedules are used to collect monitoring and evaluation data from representative samples of people involved in or affected by the use of audio — e.g. students, tutors and facilitators. This data is recorded, analysed and interpreted — often with the aid of computers and statistical techniques — and forms the basis of monitoring and evaluation reports. These reports present and analyse the data, draw out its implications and usually make recommendations for improving the system.

— *Focus groups* — a method widely used in marketing and advertising (and increasingly in politics), which involves bringing together a representative group (e.g. in our case, students and/or tutors) to discuss in depth some aspect of the subject under review — e.g. the use of drama in non-formal education or ways of improving an audio-vision package designed for individual student use.

— *Observation* — which involves systematically watching and listening to, recording and subsequently interpreting, the behaviours of people who are either designing and producing audio, or are using the materials (individually or in groups). This type of data collection, if it is to be used seriously, requires special training. It is generally used in conjunction with other data collection methods — such as sample surveys or focus groups.

These methods can either be used individually or in combination. As a general rule, the combined use of different methods is likely to produce more valid and reliable data; and therefore provide a better and more reliable basis for suggesting and implementing changes in procedures and practices.

The last three methods outlined above can also be used by different people — by research and evaluation specialists, by subject specialists and producers, by part-time tutors and facilitators. However, if the methods are being used by non-specialist staff, it always makes sense to take advice from people with knowledge and experience of research and evaluation, either internally or from another institution or project. Such people can provide useful advice on, for instance:

— The design of questionnaires, interview schedules and observation schemes

— Their use in data collection, subsequent analysis and interpretation.— The selection of samples and the setting up of focus groups

— The preparation and presentation of reports and recommendations

Research and evaluation data does not interpret itself; nor does it tell you directly what action needs to be taken. Merely collecting the data is not enough. Data has to be analysed and interpreted. And this interpretation needs to lead to action — action for change and improvement in distance and open learning systems and in our case action to improve the impact and effectiveness of audio. Evaluation without action is no evaluation at all; it is merely rhetoric. Different methods of monitoring and evaluation are appropriate for different stages of the audio process.

Planning

At the planning stage, both for institutional planning and the overall planning of audio in support of particular courses, internal review and external assessment and advice are important. Those involved in policy making, resource allocation, planning and scheduling need to establish clear targets and performance criteria. They need to review progress and achievements regularly and take remedial action where necessary. In relatively new institutions or projects, or situations where new planning systems are being introduced, it is also useful to seek external advice and assistance. There is now a good deal of relevant international experience and expertise in the setting up and operation of structures and processes for planning in distance and open learning, both at the institutional level and in terms of course planning. Each institution or project will need to develop its own procedures and practices in this area. But it would be unwise not to have them monitored and evaluated as they develop by external experts with access to a wider range of appropriate international experience.

Design and development

In designing and developing audio materials, it is important to monitor and evaluate both the 'products' that are being developed and the 'process' through which this is taking place. There are three main ways in which the quality of audio materials can be monitored and evaluated as they are emerging during the design and development process:

— *Peer review* — in which audio materials (usually in detailed outline or draft script form) are reviewed and commented on by one or more fellow members of a course team

— *Critical reading* — similar to peer review, but involving subject specialists and producers who are specifically asked to review emerging material and offer constructive criticism and suggestions for improvement

— *External assessment* — a more formal review of emerging materials by a specially appointed 'external assessor', usually a senior figure from another comparable institution or project, who is responsible for ensuring the quality and acceptability of the material.

These procedures have emerged mainly in relation to the development of printed materials in distance and open learning. They are more difficult to apply to audio, because of the way audio is developed and produced. Nevertheless, in the interest of quality, it is worth exposing initial audio ideas, series outlines and draft scripts to this kind of critical review, which needs to involve both subject specialists and producers.

In addition, it is also worth 'pre-testing' materials, both audio and printed support, as they are being designed and developed, particularly if they are using new approaches which you have not tried before. It is difficult to say exactly when pre-testing should take place — i.e. whether it should be part of the development process, or come early in the production phase. In addition to monitoring and evaluating emerging audio 'products', it is also important to be self-critical about the design and development 'process'.

Production

The production phase for audio grows out of the design and development phase. It involves transforming a set of ideas for audio into finished radio programmes, audio cassettes or audio-vision packages, ready for distribution and student use. Since production is a continuation of design and development, most of the methods and approaches to monitoring and evaluation discussed above are continued into the production phase. And again attention has to be paid to both 'products' and 'processes'. As far as 'process' is concerned, our earlier discussion identified a number of key areas and activities that need to be monitored and evaluated in relation to audio production. In particular:

— equipment and facilities

— producer workloads

— budgets and use of resources

— production scheduling

— staffing provision — management of recording

— skill levels and training needs

— professional and technical standards

The managers of audio production and the production of associated materials they need to:

— Establish and promote good working practices and standards of performance

— Measure activities and achievements against these norms and expectations

— Identify areas in which performance falls short of professional requirements

— Take remedial action to ensure and maintain high standards of output

As in other areas, these responsibilities can only be carried out within a 'culture of quality' which reflects a shared commitment to a set of professional values that involves all staff in a continuing process of aiming for and achieving the highest standards of production. The 'products' of the production stage are radio programmes, audio cassettes and audio-vision packages, ready to be broadcast or distributed to students and ready for student use. Once again, it is important to monitor and evaluate the quality of these 'finished' materials.

To some extent, this can be achieved, as at the design and development stage, through peer review, critical listening/viewing and expert assessment. However, although these methods are still useful, now that the audio materials are in recorded form, it is possible to take the process further. It is possible to go beyond making judgements about professional credibility and instructional design, and begin to look at the educational effectiveness of materials as they are being used by students. This process is normally called 'developmental testing' or 'formative evaluation'.

The main aim of developmental testing/formative evaluation is to monitor and evaluate the use of selected audio and associated print materials — usually those developed early in the production process for a course — so that the findings of the evaluation can be fed back into the development and production of later materials in order to improve their quality and effectiveness. It is usual, therefore, for course teams to select one or two fairly typical examples of radio programmes or audio cassette materials from the early part of a course; to subject them to developmental testing/formative evaluation; and to feed back the results into the production process, so that later materials are improved.

The approach and methods used for developmental testing/formative evaluation are essentially the same as those suggested earlier for 'pre-testing'. The main difference is that now you are dealing with a complete audio-based learning package. In addition to the audio material, this will usually involve — particularly for formal courses:

— Preparatory work on the relevant parts of the course text(s)

— Learning activities linked to the use of the audio or audio-visual material

— Follow-up activities design to reinforce knowledge and skills acquired from audio

Distribution

The 'product' of distribution is the successful delivery of radioprogrammes and/or audio cassettes, together with support material, to distance and open learning students. Its 'process' usually requires cooperation with a number of different organisations. For instance:

— The broadcasting agencies responsible for transmitting radio programmes

— The postal services or couriers who deliver cassettes and support material to students

— Local study centre staff — if they are involved in passing on materials to students and/or providing listening facilities

All of these operations need to be monitored and evaluated on a regular basis. Performance criteria need to be established. The efficiency and effectiveness of delivery systems need to be measured and assessed. Where performance falls short of what is required, remedial action needs to be taken.

The responsibility for monitoring and evaluation of distribution and delivery systems will usually be shared among a number of different individuals and organisations:

— Those who develop and produce the materials

— Those involved in storing materials, collating and packing them for distribution

— Those responsible for broadcast transmission or physical distribution

— Those involved in the distribution and use of materials at the local level.

Detailed arrangements will obviously vary from institution to institution and from project to project. However, in most cases, because of the range of different organisations involved, it makes sense to identify one person with overall responsibility for coordinating the monitoring and evaluation of the distribution process.

The main methods employed are likely to be the direct observation of the distribution process — with careful recording of faults in the system and responses to them — and regular sample surveys of students and tutors/facilitators about their experience of receiving audio and other materials. The surveys should reveal the nature and extent of any problems in distribution. Observation should identify the causes of the problems and suggest appropriate remedial action.

Monitoring student's use

Monitoring and evaluating the particular contribution of audio materials to student learning — i.e. the 'product' of audio in use — is generally quite difficult. The main reason for this is that, in most distance and open learning systems, audio is only one of a number of media which students are using. In well designed systems, the use of audio is closely integrated with the use of print and other media and learning activities. As a result, it is difficult to separate out the specific contribution of audio, and distinguish it from that of print and other media. However, there are a number of indirect ways in which the impact and effectiveness of audio can be measured, and from which we can draw inferences about the level of satisfaction with the medium and its probable contribution to the process of teaching and learning. Some of the more important indicators are suggested below.

— The extent to which students listen to radio programmes when they are broadcast, and make use of audio cassettes either individually or in groups

— Students' judgements about the value of audio materials as part of their study activities, and their views on the contribution audio makes to their learning

— The views of teaching staff, tutors and facilitators on student attitudes to the audio materials that form part of their courses

— Their observations of student reactions and responses to audio — e.g. levels of use at local study centres, indications of audio in assignments and examinations

The main ways of obtaining information like this are through the use of sample surveys, interviews and discussions with students, tutors and facilitators, and reports from full- and part-time staff at local centres.

Surveys: One simple and effective way of obtaining survey data is to include an audio evaluation form with students' printed course materials or audio notes. This form can ask the sort of questions suggested earlier — in the discussion of formative evaluation. This technique can also be used as a source of data for 'piloting' audio materials — i.e. trying out and evaluating audio material the first time a course is offered, with a view to revising and improving it for subsequent presentations — and as a source of data for broader 'summative evaluations' of courses.

Interviews and discussions: There are usually plenty of opportunities for local staff to meet with students to discuss their reactions to using audio. Such contacts are often more difficult for course development and production staff; and there is always a danger that they can become out of touch with their students. One way of overcoming this is for central staff to visit local centres as often as possible — e.g. when they are pre-testing or formatively evaluating materials, or in connection with the recruitment, selection and training of local tutors or facilitators. In addition, residential courses and weekend schools provide useful opportunities for holding focused discussion with students and tutors about audio — and of course other media!

Local networks: Many institutions and projects have well developed local networks of study and resource centres. It is important to make use of these networks for monitoring and evaluating audio. Local centres — and also the networks offered by government agencies and NGOs — not only provide a way of distributing materials and information, they also allow the systematic collection of feedback on course materials and study activities throughout your area. For these networks to work well, clear areas of responsibility need to be defined at central and local levels; and channels of communication need to be opened and maintained between levels. Establishing and sustaining such networks takes time and effort; but the rewards in terms of feedback on our professional activity are substantial.

Establishing priorities: For most educational institutions and projects, especially in relatively new institutions, time and effort are at a premium, and resources tend to be in short supply. In terms of monitoring and evaluating audio, it is therefore essential to establish priorities. It will not be possible to do everything — so what are the most important tasks to be undertaken and how should you approach them? Rather than offering a suggested answer to this question, it makes more sense to invite you to think about it for yourself.

5

Lifelong Distance Learning

Information is basically data, which with the addition of learning becomes knowledge. In other words learning which is based on the capacity to find, access, apply and transform information into new knowledge. Important competencies which learners require to make this transformation are often called information literacy competencies and include awareness of the need for information, the ability to critically analyse information and evaluate its usefulness and ultimately to be able to apply the information, turning it into knowledge. Communication is that simple act of dialogue between peoples and cultures that takes on a new dimension when combined with 'information' and 'technology'.

Technology is not strictly limited to the Internet and includes simpler technology such as CDROM, video, television etc although the term 'information technology' does imply the use of the Internet and telecommunication networks. Certainly in educational practices, information technology falls into two parts:

1. computer technology which is computer based courses, computerised tests, word processors, graphics software, spreadsheets, databases and presentation software.
2. telecommunications software which offers distance courses, distributed educational resources, e-mail, videoconferencing, bulleting boards, whiteboards and chat.'

The application of ICT can take many forms and has the ability to 'revolutionise the way teaching and learning occurs. The concurrent use of multimedia and computers permits the development of new pedagogical approaches involving active and interactive learning' e.g. using computer based learning methods, problem based learning, project based learning, online, video conferencing, satellite links.

ICT can lead to interactive, constantly changing, two way, customised or individualised teaching and learning which allows users to do things with information and make something new - 'print is read, online is used; print is studied, online is making; print is knowing, online is doing.'

With the increased use of ICT as a means of instruction, 'the decreased importance of physical distance means that the best (and the worst educational and corporate institutions) of any country can decide to open a branch anywhere in the world or to reach out across borders using the Internet or satellite communication links, effectively competing with any national university on its own territory.' This has advantages and disadvantages which raises further challenges to us – advantages if a nation is not able to finance educational opportunities within its borders and can access appropriate.educational systems in this way. The disadvantages however are very real - how do students determine which is the best course for them, and what are the challenges for governments to ensure appropriate accreditation and evaluation processes are in place to ensure these programs and degrees meet acceptable academic and professional standards?

Sharing expertise is an important component of nations' aid programs and an interesting example is the Virtual Colombo Plan. The Plan intends to make intensive use of ICT. This is a joint World Bank and Australian Government project which will inject A$200 million over 5 years into supporting a project to assist the development of basic education, educational infrastructure, information dissemination and higher education. This will take the form of:

— scholarships each year to support distance education programs (using the Internet in many cases) for training and up skilling primary school teachers

— establishment of eight multi purpose teacher education learning centres in Teachers Colleges in PNG (equipped with computers and communication equipment)

— development of content for delivery through the African Virtual University

— assistance to developing countries in the development of policies and strategies which will maximise the benefits of the use of ICT

— extend the World Bank's information technology network into developing countries

Changes in the environment in which education operates, particularly, the demands educational systems are receiving from both their students and the workplace.

The increasing diversity of use of ICT in industry is placing proportional demands for ICT to be integrated across the courses that we offer. Also, 'from the student's perspective, the desire to position oneself for the new types of jobs in the knowledge economy provides a strong incentive to mix study program options and qualifications, often beyond the traditional institutional boundaries. New patterns of demand are emerging, whereby learners attend several institutions or programs in parallel or sequentially, thus defining their own skill profiles on the labour market.'

Educating the global village raises a number of challenges for the education industry. Just as the 'impact of global competition and the ability of industries, organisations and individuals to adapt to new and evolving business environments will be the key determinant in maintaining a sustainable business future', so, for our students will be the importance of their ability to adapt and obtain qualifications which are relevant and useful in the 21 st century.

Using ICT for quality teaching, learning and effective management revolves around issues that can be categorised as the 'five Ps - practical, pedagogical, policy, philosophical and personal'.

1) *Practical factors.* In summary practical issues include two related categories – financial and infrastructure.

   The financial implications include:

   a) Capital required to establish an ICT infrastructure including quite high initial costs of hardware and software etc. The increased use of multimedia means that more high-end equipment, software and peripherals are required and that the aging infrastructure needed a major upgrade. The practice of purchasing one new computer and passing the older ones down the line to other staff or students is no longer acceptable. The economics of this new approach is significant and will impact on the overall financial position of the Institute. Leasing options must be a major consideration.

b) Funding required to train staff and to release them from normal duties for training.

c) Funding required to be able to pay computer teachers and support staff the equivalent to what they would receive in the market place.

d) What is the best and affordable means to provide student access to technology – should the institution lend or perhaps even subsidise the purchase of equipment? How are the funding implications of this practice met? What is the overall infrastructure investment required and how can this be funded?

e) Issues of intellectual property and copyright, particularly the cost of adapting materials into, for example, online formats and providing access to resources online.

Infrastructure requirements include:

a) Changes to facilities and perhaps even the purchase of new furniture to provide appropriate physical access and meet occupational health and safety standards – including any special airconditioning requirements.

b) Provision of a reliable electrical supply.

c) Changes which may be required in classroom layouts to accommodate more flexible learning, for example, combining online and regular classroom courses gives students more opportunity for human interaction and the development of the social aspects of learning but this can have quite large impacts on the provision of appropriate spaces and technology support.

d) Establishment of special units for the development of ICT enhanced courses and materials, online development etc.

e) Rethinking how traditional student and staff support services will be provided.

2) *Pedagogical issues:* The use of ICT needs to be tempered with reference to sound pedagogical principles. The Web is the latest in a long line of technology that can be used for teaching and learning and it coincides with change at universities teaching approaches. We need to be reflective about the direction and the nature of such change and to keep the focus on pedagogical concerns. The discussions held in Jomtien earlier this year at the Education International conference resulted in recommendations that provide a basis for discussion on the use of appropriate technologies and methodologies. In essence there was a clear message from Jomtien that educational practice needs to keep pace with appropriate technology 'as a means of improving education' but not at the expense of further denying the right of access to education by all. There is no argument that to live and work in an ICT dominated world, learners need to graduate with competencies

which will ensure that they are critical thinkers and competent problem solvers and able to analyse, interpret, evaluate and apply information to vastly different systems. This raises a range of pedagogical issues for school, vocational education and universities including:

a) facilitating an integrated, collaborative approach to teaching and learning. Using the Internet alone will not ensure that this happens - to be truly effective we need to ensure that our students also have access to interdisciplinary skills across the curriculum. To implement this may require changes in how teaching and learning occurs with, for example, much more collaboration between teachers of all disciplines. Integrating learning across the curriculum can also involve the community as a learning environment.

b) using ICT to enhance learning by catering for individual learning styles, allowing learners to make connections with knowledge and analyse, explain and apply knowledge to practical applications, make decisions and work cooperatively. The Internet 'seems to have considerable potential to be able to meet this challenge because of its ability to assist with the individualisation of instruction.' (Fetherston p5) Constructivist approaches to teaching and learning with increased emphasis on personal meaning and application of knowledge places increased demands on students and teachers and the way in which learning occurs.

c) selecting and combining different media that suits students' learning styles, for example, using the technical features of the web to the advantage of teaching and learning activities.

e) the Internet needs to be regarded not just as a delivery medium, especially for distance education, but as a potential teaching and learning tool for all students across education sectors

f) impact on teachers

— ICT facilitates a more interactive approach

— teachers' ability to change their practices

3) *Personal issues* for teachers as a result of the changing demands which ICT facilitated teaching places on teachers.

The challenges for teachers include:

a) understanding their need to embrace and keep up to date with technology and its application to educational practice. 'To create a more active and interactive learning environment, faculty must have a clear vision as to the purpose of the new technologies and the most effective way of integrating them in their program design and delivery must educate themselves in the use of the new pedagogical channels and supports.

b) acceptance of pedagogical change, moving from being 'one-way' instructors towards becoming facilitators of learning

c) they will need support as they undergo personal, social and professional change

d) the need for greater flexibility in use of staff may impact on issues such as working conditions and tenure etc.

e) perceptions of teachers and their role by students. Because of the impact of the media and the Internet, students spend more time in front of the computer and TV than at school, less effort required to absorb new facts etc, 'teachers and schools, having thus lost their leading place in the learning experience, face the new tasks of making school more appealing to children while implicitly providing them with a "users' guide" to the media.')

f) communities challenging decisions regarding curriculum and being more involved in school organisation Professional development is a key strategy for teachers.

Policy issues: For ICT to be successfully implemented within the organisation, a solid underpinning of mutually reinforcing strategies and initiatives is required. These may be informed by government as well as a result of institutional policy and planning. The ICT initiatives for compulsory education in South Australia is founded in the States' information economy policies and the Department of Education, Training and Employment's own policy directions documents. For the State, the imperatives are seen to be:

— engagement and participation

— capturing attention

— stimulating imagination

— connecting people.

— linking to specific initiatives to achieve these outcomes.

Non-formal education can take many forms including corporate training (self and/or employer funded), continuing education and what we used to call leisure education. ICT is also impacting in these arenas. Just using the Internet itself is a non-formal learning experience.

In Australia the University of the third age online (U3A) is aimed to provide educational stimulus and support for older people. These are communities of people who come together to learn from one another, sometimes describes as 'a learning co-operative of older people'. It encourages positive ageing by enabling its members to share many educational, creative and leisure activities.

Life at work in the information economy outlines some very interesting examples of the use of ICT in what could be considered part of the non-formal education sector as they all involve learning of some kind. Examples include use of ICT by women in call centres, telecentres and outsourced work such as medical transcription and software services. The report cites case studies of where new technologies and networking have empowered women to access learning opportunities and to improve their social and economic status and to challenge discrimination and overcome gender barriers. These include women. in:

— Uganda – Sapphire Women who sell their crafts over the Internet

— Bangladesh, - Grameen Bank funded mobile phone services

— India – SEWA computer awareness and using the Internet courses which have led to members selling crafts through their own web sites.

Lifelong Distance Learning: Challenges of Access

Lifelong learning is now widely recognised as providing the broad framework for educational policies, whereas much of the interest in ICT in countries has concentrated on investments in schooling, with little attention to learning issues that arise in other settings and for other age groups. The *digital divid*e, a term of growing currency that captures succinctly the differential access to and use of ICT in today's world. The digital divide should be seen not primarily in technological terms, but as embedded in broader inequalities in education and learning.

In the broad context of social and technological change, there is need to explore the nature of learning inequalities, for the young and for adults, in formal and non-formal learning settings, within and across countries. This will give a better understanding of how groups within society become and remain educationally disadvantaged. Consideration can be given to the various dimensions of *learning gaps* - how they arise and are perpetuated over time - and the circumstances in which ICT can mitigate disadvantages rather than exacerbate them. Research on the educationally disadvantaged, and measures which have been activated or proposed to alleviate the problems, can illustrate the range of relevant policy considerations and options.

There is evidence to show enormous variation in computer access and familiarity within and across countries. Lack of access to ICT- the *digital divide* -has imposed new barriers on those children from poorer (and sometimes dysfunctional) homes, who are already underprivileged. In a number of countries, there is a widening gap between whole communities, according to their levels of affluence, that often works to the disadvantage of ethnic and linguistic minorities. A new dimension is brought to the notion of exclusion, as those who were already disadvantaged become yet more so through lack of computer literacy. The term *information underclass* has been coined, in awareness that those societal groups with the greatest needs may be those which get the least access to ICT.

Some schools are well equipped with ICT and make extensive and effective use of computers to enhance the quality of the learning experiences they provide across the curriculum. Their teachers may be confident and discerning in computer use. Other schools are poorly equipped with ICT and their teachers may be poorly trained to adopt ICT techniques. Problems may arise with transfer from a school rich in ICT to another that is not.

The opportunities for post-school learning vary enormously - whether in post-school training or adult education, at home or the workplace, in leisure opportunities. Various socio-economic and demographic parameters can be critical. While much is currently invested in ICT for higher education, relatively little is known about ICT as related to disadvantaged adults. As shown in different OECD surveys, there is a significant portion of the adult population in all countries in need of improved basic skills; in some countries very many face severe problems.

There are many cross-cutting issues to be addressed. For example, hardware and software continue to evolve rapidly, while the relationships between educators and technology specialists are often tenuous. Too often, we do not have a good understanding of the *consumer* in unreached populations, particularly among the most severely disadvantaged whether in OECD or non-OECD countries, nor of the effectiveness of different ICT-based strategies to reach these populations. There are the inter-generational issues, for example, in early childhood use of ICT as well as use by older adults in their *third age*.

Schools throughout the industrialised world are rapidly moving to incorporate technology and to subscribe to methods of teaching that allow students considerable freedom to search, to explore and to collaborate with other students. With the skills acquired from these forms of schooling, students will be better prepared for jobs that require technology skills, information searching, and collaboration - jobs that tend to pay quite well - and to be better prepared for college where today computer skills are mandatory. If, as some studies claim, students are more motivated to attend school and to study when they have access to modern computers and the Internet, then a secondary advantage accrues to those within technology-rich schools.

Some deny the existence of a digital divide, regarding the concept as profoundly negative, a diversion from the enormous potential of ICT to open horizons and access to knowledge and information. The hope appears to be that enthusiastic affirmation of the benefits of ICT will be enough to ensure its widespread adoption.

Without careful analysis, many aspects of this divide may remain undetected, such as those relating to private computer and Internet use; the difficulty of disentangling actual from imputed educational value; the intrinsic invisibility of the "very hard to reach". Most importantly, perhaps, unequal ICT distribution may be exacerbating stubborn, long-standing educational inequalities, meaning that explicit action is required to offset a worsening situation.

Children in various groups in society have varying access to ICT, and schools therefore have an essential compensatory function. Since knowledge of ICT is necessary for the future labour market and generally strengthens people's position in society, all pupils must become sufficiently familiar with ICT. This presupposes that every school has good access to computers, and that the teachers are well in command of the educational uses of ICT.

Evidently there is no single, clearly defined "learning technology gap" or digital divide. There are many overlapping gaps, which largely do not have their roots in the technology itself. They include:

— The gaps that exist *in ICT skills, confidence and competence* between many different groups in society, gaps that can be critical to the ability to benefit from the different available educational, social and economic opportunities;

— The ICT gaps that exist *within formal education*, between one school or school district and another, in terms of the equipment, materials, connectivity, professional competence, and integration of ICT within the teaching/learning environment;

— The gaps that exist between *the home and the school*, in particular regarding the ability of some individuals and social groups to extend their existing advantages, through the additional learning resources of home computer and Internet use.

— The wide differences that exist in the integration of ICT into different forms of *tertiary education*, including distance learning which is built on the capacity of technology to open access across time and space;

— There are the digital divides in *non-formal learning settings*, some work and community settings being "technology-rich", others "technology-poor";

— *Inter-generational technology gaps* can be especially important when the focus is on participation in the economy and society, and on lifelong learning;

— There are the very wide *national disparities*, between the richest countries of the world, including the US to which most of the existing data relate, and other countries, with much lower or minimal technology use in education, homes, enterprises and communities.

Disparities in access to ICT in America are highly related to race, income and education demographics. For example, Black and Hispanic households are less than half as likely as white households to have Internet access. Also, households with higher levels of education among adults are far more likely to own computers and have Internet access than those at the lowest education levels. In 1998, for example, only 7.9% of households with an elementary education degree, and 15.7% of households with some high school education, had personal computers; however, 31.2% of households with a high school diploma had computers at home.

There are important divides that exist between well-resourced and poor communities, even in near proximity one to another. Of particular concern in many countries are the linguistic gaps, especially given the software and Internet dominance of English.

A further typology offered for understanding different ICT access issues for education and learning was:

- — Those with special needs or physical disability;
- — The socially and economically deprived;
- — Linguistic and ethnic minorities;
- — Groups suffering social exclusion;
- — The geographically remote;
- — Older citizens, for whom new technology has arrived late in life;
- — The technologically-alienated or apathetic.

These categorisations overlap, and are incomplete, so they are illustrative rather than exhaustive. It will be important to develop convincing frameworks for the analysis of the educational digital divide, recognising that there will always be different ways of categorising problems, as well as differences in conditions and priorities between countries.

The root causes of the digital divide include, among other factors: geography, racism, chauvinism, colonialism, imperialism, ethnic conflict, religious and cultural beliefs and practices, poverty (lack of investment capital), the absence of key infrastructures of education and human capital (knowledge) and the failure to develop traditions of speech freedoms and scientific inquiry that are generally associated with the highly industrialised nations...The digital divide, thus, is more than just the physical distance between those who have access and those who do not. It is really the measure of the distance of the gaps of power, wealth, of knowledge, data, good health care, sound nutrition, access to the good life. There is also a psychological distance in the digital divide. Nations, regions within nations and continents, individuals also account for the space between the digital divide.

Of all the different manifestations of the digital divide - in commerce, the media, public administration, etc. - perhaps the most important concerns education and learning, in so far as the fundamental role of ICT in contemporary life is itself dependent on knowledge, competence and expertise.

general terms, ICT [techniques] applied to education have an intrinsic compensatory nature. This is due to the massive reach they have and to the homogeneous quality that can be achieved. Their capability to reach massive audiences and offer equal quality of content throughout, coupled with their capacity to target groups with specialised needs, is a crucial attribute they bring to education... This is particularly so in developing countries, where rural areas and ample sectors of the urban population have little access to information and educational services. The potential benefits of ICT externalities are clearly more powerful than in developed countries. The social returns are higher because, in all likelihood, there will be more people who benefit from them in more ways.

It would be convenient if the policy issues related to the digital divide could be understood as a set of recipes for improvement which countries could implement to a greater or lesser degree. It is clear, however, that the reality is both more complex and dynamic than any simple model allows. Diverse conditions and cultures rule out simplicity. Many stakeholders are involved, and some of the most pertinent variables are the furthest from policy influence, including those related to community and household practices.

Dilemmas arise at very general levels, as well as in specific fields. Education, learning and the acquisition of knowledge and skills have never been more central than they are today, and will most likely be yet more important in years to come.

The strong links between learning and the "economic health" of individuals through human capital investment are now widely acknowledged, and parallel lessons can be drawn for enterprises as "learning organisations", as well as for entire industries, geographical areas and national economies. While these developments are frequently seen as positive features of post-industrialised society, they have a negative side: the consequences for those individuals, organisations or communities that fall behind in learning become the more profound, and can be dire. The process of creating "winners" often creates "losers".

The rapid growth in equipping schools with computers and Internet connectivity has resulted in much more even school access, making the digital divide related to out-of-school home access the more crucial. This in turn raises the key issue of how far the education system can play a compensatory role, as suggested in certain of the quotations reproduced here, or whether existing inequalities in schools might be exacerbated, even when investments are evenly spread . It is an aspect of the digital divide that perhaps deserves closer research attention.

The digital divide among adults within and across many nations is likely to persist for many years to come, and is probably more resistant to change than that amongst children and youth, who will be growing up within societies ever more permeated by new technologies. Further, the vast majority of ICT investments in education have gone into K-12 and higher education, up until now bypassing the educational needs of disadvantaged adults world-wide. Nonetheless, the converse of this relatively sober assessment is that there are, in various ways, extraordinary opportunities for ICT to make a real difference in low-literate and adult populations. This conclusion is a result of the often greater flexibility of programming for adult education, which is less hampered by rigid state education systems, required curricula, and constraints on individual motivation. In sum, the greater the divide or gap, the more dramatic the leap can be.

The position of the teacher is seen to be pivotal, for the quality implementation of ICT strategies in education to bridge different divides, though they can have a negative influence in creating or reinforcing divides as well. Teacher education and professional development questions should be to the fore. Despite the appearance of ever-cheaper technologies, the cost issue is and will remain critical, especially for developing countries and communities.

Linguistic issues are certainly important in many countries, given the dominance of the English language in software and the Internet. Cultural diversity is one reason behind interest in these issues, but so is the avoidance of social exclusion among non-English-speaking populations.

There is a general perception that evaluation tends to be under-developed. Lack of evaluation may be linked to the speed of change, as well as to the nature of high-profile initiatives that are politically driven and so implemented no matter what the results of evaluation. In these cases, there may be a valuable role for research and evaluation in indicating how the committed resources can best be deployed.

6

Distance Education Development in India

Ever since university education was introduced in India in 1857, its quality has remained generally intractable. It is true that well-meaning educators have, from time to time, expressed their concerns about its quality, but, by and large, the overall dynamics of education have been governed by market forces—mainly the vast gap between supply and demand.

After independence in 1947, a conceptual shift from quality control to quality assurance was noticed. Efforts made to improve the quality of education through inputs like streamlined funding, appropriate infrastructure, and relevant guidelines pointed to a new guiding assumption, that if the quality of the inputs improved, then the quality of education stood assured. Reality, however, did not seem to confirm this stimulus–response relationship.

Efforts to overcome the weaknesses of the education system were started in earnest with the Education Commission, which assumed that quality assurance was a consequence of adequate inputs. Some of the major steps taken are manifest in the following:

— the establishment of the University Grants Commission (UGC) in 1956;

— the Association of Indian universities;

— the various State Boards of secondary and higher secondary education;

— the Central Board of secondary and higher secondary education;

— the National Council of Educational Research and Training;

— the Asian Institute of Educational Planning and Administration; and

— the establishment of Academic Staff Colleges to provide orientation and refresher programmes for the junior academic staff of colleges and universities..

At the level of higher education, the following measures were seen as sufficient to ensure quality in education:

— prescribing qualifications for various personnel to be employed;

— fixing the minimum levels of infrastructure in terms of land, buildings, classrooms, laboratories, furniture, equipment, libraries, and so on;

— providing guidelines for the content and conduct of syllabuses and examinations;

— providing funds and grants in aid for the promotion and development of new subject areas; and

— establishing new institutions.

At the secondary and higher secondary levels, the key to quality assurance continued to be seen in reforming, upgrading, and updating the syllabuses and examinations, as well as enforcing strict adherence to recruitment norms. These measures instilled confidence and for a while it was felt that the quality of education in India had been secured for the future.

The corresponding expansion of education and the speed with which students entered at all levels of admission, together with the rising aspirations of newly awakened populations of diverse learner communities, however, opened the way for independent institutions and unrecognised universities that would neither depend on the University Grants Council for grants, nor observe the necessary conditions to make their operations legally valid.

Recently, with the establishment of open and distance education, the issue of quality has become more serious. Partly because distance education institutions launched courses without any reasonable understanding of the distance education system, very often without sufficiently preparing for effective distance education transactions, the questioned perception that distance education could provide an effective teaching–learning environment and the issue of falling standards came to the fore when the practices and principles of conventional and distance education were compared.

The initial reaction of distance educators in India manifested in their building a defence for distance education as an effective educational system, as if quality was an issue only for distance education systems and not for the conventional system. The perceived effectiveness of conventional education was used as a standard measure for the effectiveness of distance education.

Distance education expanded with an overwhelming momentum, both in its use and misuse, as teacher training and science-based programmes began to multiply rapidly on the one hand and professional–vocational and awareness–extension programmes expanded on the other. The debate become broad based as the validity of using conventional notions of effectiveness as a measure for the effectiveness of distance education came to be questioned. The attention of those concerned shifted slowly but steadily from mere perception to the reality—hardly anything in concrete terms could be characterised as a quality assurance mechanism in the Indian educational system, be it conventional education or distance education.

The UGC has realised as well that they play a recommendatory and funding role and that, if an institution can mobilise funds independently, it will not bother about UGC recommendations and guidelines. It was time the issue of quality in education was addressed afresh. This brings us to the latest thinking on and the steps taken to achieve quality in education. Rather than depending on the assumption that quality is assured by ensuring inputs, the paradigm of the 1990s is that quality can be assured only when all the processes involved are ensured through appropriate management—not assumptions but appropriate activities ensure quality.

Accordingly, the National Assessment and Accreditation Council (NAAC) was established within the UGC to plan and implement schemes for ensuring quality in higher education. For distance education operations in India, the Distance Education Council within Indira Gandhi National Open University (IGNOU) is expected to take this responsibility and work in close collaboration with NAAC. Both bodies, however, have as yet taken only what may be called the initial steps.

At present seven open universities operate in India. Of these, two state open universities have yet to start operating; another two have started operating but they have not reached a stage when their quality assurance practices and principles could be looked into. The remaining three universities are Dr. B. R. Ambedkar Open University (BRAOU) of Andhra Pradesh (1982), Indira Gandhi National Open University (IGNOU) of Ne w Delhi (1985), and Yashwantrao Chavan Maharashtra Open University (YCMOU)) of Maharashtra (1989).

It is clear from the organisational structures of BRAOU and IGNOU that they have no mechanisms provided explicitly for quality assurance. The tasks involved, however, make it necessary to incorporate various mechanisms which may be labelled *quality assurance scheme* at the conceptual level and *quality assurance operations* at the implementation level.

Dr. B. R. Ambedkar Open University (BRAOU)

The main function of BRAOU is the preparation and delivery of educational programmes. Accordingly, quality assurance measures are related to the following six processes:

— planning academic programmes;

— developing curricula and learning materials;

— producing learning materials;

— implementing programmes;

— reviewing programmes; and

— developing human resources.

New academic programmes are usually identified with the vice-chancellor through informal discussions with and suggestions or guidelines received from the state government, the UGC, and other national bodies. Faculty may also initiate proposals. Proposals initiated by either the vice-chancellor or faculty are placed before the co-ordination committee, which is a non-statutory advisory body made up all senior functionaries like the deans of the various faculties and directors of the various service units.

After the co-ordination committee approves the proposal, the faculty or department prepares a detailed proposal for the consideration of the academic senate, the highest statutory academic authority of the university that is empowered to approve academic programmes. The detailed proposals approved at this stage are submitted to the executive council, the highest policy making and administrative authority of the university, for administrative sanction to launch the programmes. The vice-chancellor, the faculty, the co-ordination committee, the academic senate, and the executive council, all serve as a means of assuring the relevance and quality of the programmes at the planning stage.

After a programme is finally approved, an expert committee made up of the internal faculty members and external subject experts is constituted to prepare the curriculum. The committee may meet once or twice for this purpose, and the curriculum thus designed is sent for approval to the academic senate. Thus, it is the subject experts and the academic senate who look into the quality of the programme at this stage.

The approved curriculum and syllabus are passed on to the course team, which consists of subject experts (both from the university and from outside institutions) and an audio-visual producer, who is designated for the programme or course. The team is headed by a subject expert, who is designated the editor and is responsible for content editing and the quality of presentation. Language is edited by language experts. The course team also identifies the audio-visual components of the materials, which are developed by the audio-visual centre with the help of the producer and subject experts.

Depending on the nature of the course or programme, field practitioners are also associated with the development of learning materials as course writers, editors, or audio-visual programme developers. In a few cases, the p rint materials are sent to external assessors for their comments, which are subsequently used to improve the materials. The audio-visual materials are previewed by the internal faculty before they are duplicated for use by students.

The quality assurance mechanisms that function at this stage include:

— editing learning materials for different purposes (content, format, and language);

— co-ordinating with the producer of audio-visual materials and previewing the audio -visual materials before they are duplicated; and

— orienting the course writers to make them familiar with the requirements of quality.

The learning materials in manuscript form are printed by the material production division of the university with the help of private printing agencies. They follow a style manual that the university prepared with the help of printers and internal faculty members. Internal faculty read the final proofs to ensure error free publications. Similarly, the audio-visual unit is responsible for producing the audio-visual tapes in accordance with an audio-visual manual prepared by the university. Thus the internal faculty, the audio-visual unit, and the printing division are collectively responsible for the quality of print and media learning materials at the production stage.

When a course is implemented, the three main processes are distributing learning materials, providing student support services, and issuing examinations. Learning materials are distributed from the material distribution division at headquarters, and they are responsible for preparing and adhering to despatch schedules. Student support services are provided by a network of study centres at different locations. The directorate of student services located at headquarters is responsible for ensuring the quality of these services by determining the norms and patterns of support services required at different study centres.

The examination branch of the university is responsible for the reliability and validity of evaluation. The schemes of evaluation and the conduct of examinations are developed by the faculty with the help of external experts wherever necessary, and are approved by the academic senate and the executive council before implementation.

Learning materials are reviewed on the basis of feedback from learners, counsellors, and subject experts and they are updated by internal faculty. The university has set up a separate system evaluation unit, which conducts regular studies on the different aspects of learning materials and implementation processes. The feedback from these studies is used to revise materials and improve practices.

The university has established a separate unit for staff training and development. This unit undertakes orientation and training programmes for the academic and administrative staff to improve the quality of their services.

Indira Gandhi National Open University (IGNOU)

At IGNOU, quality assurance activities focus on processes quite similar to those at BRAOU, but the measures taken to achieve the desired quality differ considerably.

Existing built-in quality assurance mechanisms are as follows:

— planning the course or programme;

— developing the course or programme;

— producing the learning materials;

— implementing the course or programme;

— reviewing the courses and follow up activities; and

— developing human resources.

Each school or division is expected to present a perspective plan covering a period of about five years. This perspective plan must be approved by the co-ordination committee and, subsequently, after incorporating the modifications the committee suggests, the perspective plan must be approved by the planning board. Within the approved perspective plan, the school or division is expected to prepare a project concept pertaining to each course or programme that they want to launch. This project concept is developed through the services of experts in the relevant field or any other means such as workshops, brainstorming sessions, and so on. The project concept is submitted to the co-ordination committee and then to the planning board for their approval. After the project concept is approved by the planning board, the school or division develops a detailed outline of the curriculum components of the course or programme. The project design must be enriched in consultation with an expert committee, made up of subject experts and instructional designers. It is then submitted to the school board for approval.

After looking into various aspects of the project design and enriching it through interaction with experts, it is finalised as a project report, which presents the total instructional design of the course or programme for the academic council to consider. While the project report is being shaped, another document called the *launch document* is developed in co-operation with the admission and evaluation division and the communication division. The launch document outlines relevant schedules as well as the infrastructure needed and the kind of services required to implement the course or programme. The launch document is also submitted to the co-ordination committee for approval.

At this point the planning stage is over. So far the mechanisms for quality assurance at the concept and design stages lie with the co-ordination committee, the planning board, the school board, and the academic council. Following these steps meticulously, the quality of the course or programme is sure to meet the objectives of the university, social relevance, economic viability, and operational feasibility.

Using the approved project report and the launch document, the school or division moves on to the stage of course or programme development. Usually, the task of co-ordinating development is given to a course or programme co-ordinator, who assists the course contributors, content editors, language editors, instructional designers, audio-visual producers, and personnel involved in the project.

Course contributors, the main constituent of this team, are usually identified with the help of an expert committee. They undergo a two-day orientation programme so that they may design materials in accordance with the house style adopted by a particular school. First drafts received from the course contributors are passed on to content editors (who are subject experts), language editors, and format editors (who are instructional designers). They look into the pedagogic and presentational attributes of the materials and make changes. The final draft is prepared and thoroughly proofread before camera-ready copies are prepared.

Besides developing the learning materials, course contributors are expected to suggest topics that need audio -visual support. These suggestions are written up as *academic briefs*, which are further developed as *academic notes*, which outline in detail the expected academic content of the audio-visual materials to be prepared. Sometimes the academic briefs and the academic notes are prepared by the course contributors; other times they may be prepared by the internal academics themselves.

The academic note is passed on to the communication division, who assign a producer to produce the programme. The producer and the academic work together to build both the script and the production script. The producer plans and arranges for the technical facilities and technical support required to produce the materials. Rushes collected from outdoor as well as indoor shooting are edited at the post production centre to finalise the first version of the audio-visual programme, which is previewed by a committee of internal academics and technical personnel. After approval the programme is passed on for duplication and packing.

The quality assurance of course or programme development, and print and audio-visual materials, therefore, relies on the following mechanisms:

- orienting the course contributors;
- content editing by subject specialists;
- language editing by language experts;
- format editing by instructional designers;
- collaborating to identify themes for audio-visual materials;
- combining academics with audio-visual producers and providing high-level technical facilities; and
- previewing the audio-visual programmes before finalising them.

The quality of learning materials production depends on the following:

- the quality of the paper on which they are printed;
- the cards in which they are bound;
- the quality of the printing itself;
- the appropriateness of layout;

— accuracy in typography; and

— the placement of diagrams.

Similarly, in the case of audio-visual materials, quality depends on the quality of blank tapes and duplication, which is carried out at the university. The mechanisms to ensure the quality of paper, card, and blank tapes are the advisory technical committees, which set the minimum standards for the quality of the materials the university is to use. The general quality of printing is assured by penalty clauses in the agreements with the printers.

A course or programme is implemented through many processes: the despatch of materials; counselling, tutoring, and practical work at study centres; assignment handling; query handling; feedback; and evaluation. The quality of these processes is assured by ensuring the prerequisites which support them as follows:

— *Despatch of materials*: availability of materials in the warehouse, availability of schedules, adherence to schedules, quality of packing;

— *Counselling, tutoring, and practical work*: availability of schedules, adherence to schedules, punctuality, regularity, availability of facilities, attendance of learners, quality of learners, quality of counselling or tutoring, practical work and interaction, use of audio-visual materials, learner satisfaction;

— *Assignment handling*: availability of schedules, adherence to schedules, short turn-around time, quality of assessment;

— *Query handling*: pre-admission services, on-course services, and post-course services;

— *Feedback on*: quality of print materials, quality of audio-visual materials, quality of counselling, tutoring, and practical work, quality of assignments, quality of support services in general; and

— *Evaluation:* availability of schedules, adherence to schedules, conduct of examinations, turn-around time in the case of assessment, handling of appeals made by the students and discipline issues, results (time taken for declaration) and their accuracy, regular and timely certification.

At study centres and regional centres, quality assurance mechanisms comprise the various monitoring schemes and related feedback mechanisms that originate there. Regional centres are expected to monitor study centres for the quality of their management, tutoring, and counselling, and their general function and facilities, while study centres provide feedback on their infrastructure, the functioning of tutors and counsellors, and learner behaviour.

Course review activities depend mainly on the feedback made available to regional centres and, in turn, to headquarters. Along with the project report at the start of the course, a review document is prepared, which outlines a timetable for receiving feedback as well as the various areas under which feedback is to be received. Feedback informs decisions about whether the course should continue (entailing preparation of new assignments and programme guides for every year), be modified (entailing maintenance of courses through supplements and minor revisions), expanded (entailing restructuring of courses and also increasing the content by means of revisions), or withdrawn (if the course is no longer relevant).

The Staff Training and Research Institute of Distance Education (STRIDE), an IGNOU constituent, provides staff development programmes for the academic and non-academic staff to improve the quality of their input.

Disatnce Education Experiecnes in IGNOU

As an apex body, IGNOU acts as a coordinating, monitoring and funding agency for the distance education system in the country. The University has constituted the Distance Education Council (DEC) for this purpose which started functioning since April 1992. The range of educational programmes of IGNOU has increased year after year. Similarly, the enrolment of students has also increased year after year. Thus the growth in academic programmes is from 03 to 39 programmes and student enrolment from 4500 to 430 thousand during 1987 to 1998 which is manifold.

The pattern of academic programmes and student enrolment reveals that there is a gradual shift from traditional programmes and diplomas to professional and vocational degrees, and diplomas. For example, majority of IGNOU students were enrolled for BDP (B.A, B.Com) whose share in the total enrolment was around 75% in 1989-90 has come down to around 43% in 1993-94 and 22% in 1995-96 and 24% in 1996-97. Contrary to this the enrolment in management programmes has increased steadily from 17.23% in 1992 to 21.8% in1994 (Manjulika and Reddy, 1996). Management and Computer programmes accounted for 48% and 11% in 1996 and 36% and 27% in 1996-97 respectively, thus management and computer programmes are accounting for 59% and 63% of the total enrolment in 1995-96 and 1996-97.

This is an indication of the gradual shift from the regular undergraduate courses to the professional/ vocational courses such as Management and Computer programmes due to compulsion in the job market. This shift is certainly remarkable and in tune with national demand for more technocrats, managers and professionals. During 1998, the enrolment of students has increased from 52,000 in 1990 to 163,390 and the total number of students on roll has crossed 430,000. The profile of students enrolled for the year 1997 reveals that 16% are from rural remote and tribal areas, 23% women and 6% SC/ST. Thus the majority of students (84%) are from urban and male (77%). 79.6% students are in the age group below 35 years. The Profile further reveal, that female enrolment has gone up from 5.2% in 1987 to 14.6%in 1992 and 23 % in 1997.

Rural representation presents a dismal picture in 1996 and 1997 with (8.3% and 16.5% respectively) when more than 60% are living in rural and remote areas in the country. The other most disadvantaged group represents around 6% in 1996 and 1997 (Table 2). Further programme-wise breakup shows that the maximum number of women and rural students are enrolled in women studies, library sciences and undergraduate BA, B.Com programmes of the university. More than three quarters of the students in management and computer programmes are from urban (i.e. major cities and state capitals), thus leaving rural areas out of reach. Similar is the case with regard to other science programmes (Table 3).

IGNOU has adopted multimedia approach to instruction such as self-instructional (print) materials (SIMs), distance tuition through assignments, video and audio programmes, teleconference sessions, limited face-to-face counselling sessions, limited television and radio programmes (on national network of Doordarshan), video programmes through cable network, and library facilities.

An analysis of multi-media instructional system of IGNOU reveals interesting developments in the use of instructional media for imparting distance education to its learners. As other open universities in the world, IGNOU also uses SIMs as its major medium. Apart from SIMs, it has also adopted audio and videocassettes, assignments, face-to-face in the first phase (1987-1989). In the second phase (1990-1992) a few more courses, especially science and basic computer programmes have been added. During this period it has introduced practicals to meet the needs of computer and science based programmes. In addition it has also added limited broadcasting (television) into its multimedia package to take distance education to all parts of the country taking the advantage of extensive television network In the third phase (1993 onwards) the University added a number of science, computers health and technological and professional programmes.

Extensive use of labs (for practicals) and specialised institutions (for fieldwork and hands on experience) were introduced taking the diverse needs of courses. Teleconferencing also has been added realising the need for reaching out to remote and rural areas, especially in the disadvantaged sections of the society. The university has provided down link facility initially in the Regional Centres mostly in state capitals, however, the facility is being extended to 163 locations by 1998. The university is the process of connecting RCs with its Headquarters through Wide Area Network (WAN).

A few VSATS have already been installed at two of IGNOU's Regional Centres and a few more are under consideration. This facility would facilitate two-way audio and video tele-conference from a few Regional/ Study Centres in the coming years. From these VSATs, the programme and information can reach every house and work place, which has access to local cable TV or computer. The University has already begun the process of keeping courseware of educational programmes and academic services on the network. This work has already started with a few computer programmes. The MEIDS (School of Management) is offering capsule programmers in the year 1998/99 for which courseware is getting ready to put it on the network. Every School will be encouraged to offer their programmes and services on the network in future.

There are 9 Schools of Studies which are responsible for the preparation and development of course materials. The University has decentralised a year back the composing and printing activities and as a result the Schools have been entrusted with the responsibility of not only writing the course materials, which is their academic activity, but also the technical job of composing and printing. Of course, in printing the Schools depend on outside printing agencies. The delivery of distance education is effected through the combined operations of many Divisions and a few Schools namely Student Registration and Evaluation, Computer, Materials Production and Distribution, Regional Services, International Schools, STRIDE and Electronic Media and Production Centre (EMPC) and Library and Documentation Centre. These divisions are supported by various other units such as Administration, and Finance Divisions, etc. However, on the forefront it is the

Regional Services Division, which coordinates the support service network established across the length and breadth of the country.

The IGNOU students are spread all over the country and are served through Regional Centres and Study Centres. Study Centres (SC) support students in independent learning by various means of educational technologies and human support. SCs are established mostly by the University at conventional universities and colleges, and in some cases a few recognised study centres have also been setup at private/semi-government institutions and NGOS. The University has also established a few sub study centres and work centres attached to a major study centres. A few of them are established at three Central jails in different provinces. The work centre was added only for conducting practical courses. There were 77 SCs in 1989, and it has gone up to 164 in 1990 and (234) in 1996. A concept viz, programme study centre has also been added in the year 1997 where both practicals and theory counselling can be organised. In brief, these are single programme based centres. Profile of Study centres reveal that most of the centres are established in major cities/ towns or District headquarters.

Very few cities,less than one lakh population have got study centres. This clearly indicates that the Taluka headquarters and other small towns in the country have not received due representation corresponding to its population. For example enrolment pattern in 1996 shows that many study centres have less than 10 students in different programmes. Similarly 30% (79) of total study centres have less than 100 students. The reasons for these imbalances are many. A few of these worth mentioning here which are non availability of infrastructure and academic expertise. Similarly, all the study centres established are not activated for all academic programmes introduced by the university, thus, leaving out small towns and taluka headquarters for professional and science and technology courses. This clearly reveals that for IGNOU programmes, especially, professional and science and technology programmes access is limited to rural students, thus, the very objective of providing opportunity for higher education to large segment of the population, especially to disadvantaged groups and individuals is not being met.

The concept of study centres has been thoroughly reviewed during 1995-96 and diversified approach has been adopted. Besides the regular Study Centres and recognised Study Centres the University has also proposed to have new types of Study Centres such as Programmes Study Centre (PSC), Multi media Learning Centre (MMLC), Distance learning Facilitator (DLF). Partner Institution(PI) etc. The diversified approach is essentially planned to reach all sections of people including those living in rural and remote areas. Various reasons can be cited for diversified approach through which the University can fulfil its objectives, especially the mandate of "Social".

The enrolment has increased, programmes and courses have multiplied and the specialised nature of facilities required began to get diversified new issues have arisen. The process of growth has led to the emergence of several new issues and concerns. Such as:

— The growth in enrolment has not been uniform across all programmes and study centres; attachment of a small number of students with study centres which has made some of these study centres non-viable.

— The present study centre network is urban biased, leaving small towns and rural areas out of reach.

— Distance to study centres and their rigid timings have in many cases made access difficult or impossible for students.

Thus the Study Centre approach alone cannot take education to the doorsteps of the students. It is therefore, necessary to rationalise and diversify the existing centres and add new channels of delivery to reach out to all sections and parts of the country. The purpose of diversification of delivery methods is not necessarily to establish more and different ways of delivery for specific programmes only. On the other hand, the purpose is to ensure how IGNOU can reach its students who are registered on any programme irrespective of their location and the facilities to which they have access. It would follow therefore that there is no delivery mechanism that is unique to any particular programme; all programmes will attempt a combination of approaches starting with course development efforts to delivery of programmes and services.

In short the emphasis in the approach and strategies towards diversification is to develop a flexible policy framework that permit a combination of different approaches accepted by the University to reach students and provide better services to them and to establish the principle that the location of a student is not a disability in accessing higher education facilities, through the distance mode and improving the quality of services through a variety of means of value addition.

For a large number of programmes offered by the IGNOU, easy access to materials and services by students remains a major problem. Admittedly, it will not be possible to bridge this gap between the University and each of its students. It would follow therefore that a large number of access points have to be set across the country so that a large number of students can avail of the services provided by the University. Such access points will have to be essentially on a scale much lower than that visualised in the study centre concept. It is in this context, that the mechanism of distance learning facilitator (DLF) becomes significant. Conceptually, therefore the Distance Learning Facilitator will correspond to a single man study centre as against the present concept of an institution as the study centre.

In addition to the diversified delivery channels the University has also expanded its teleconferencing network across the country in a big way, in the years 1997 and 1998. The objective of this mammoth expansion was to reach its large numbers of students in no time, provide an opportunity for direct interaction, with faculty and.7 other experts for immediate feedback. Before, 1997 the University had provided this facility only at its 15 Regional Centres (with two-way interactive facility using STD telephone) and 20 study centres. Mostly these receiving-end nodes were located in provincial capitals/ major cities (except 4 study centres which are located in Outback and far flung areas in four different provinces). The teleconferencing method of instruction has created a great interest and enthusiasm among students, academic counsellors and other academic and administrative staff posted at Regional Centres and study centres.

Realizing the role and the power of the media in delivering services, the University has decided to establish 127 more nodes across the country, especially for management and computer programmes in the year 1996. Accordingly a feasibility report was prepared and

125 regular study centres and two new Regional Centres were identified. The proposal mentioned that 100% of management programme activated study centres and 42 Computer programme activated study centres would be covered.

Incidentally, many of the study centres activated for management programmes are also activated for number of other programmes including computer programmes. Thus, the proposed expansion planned to cover 50% of the total regular study centres and 60% of the total students enrolled for all programmes.

Of course, 100% coverage facility has been planned for management programme. The proposal has been executed in the year 1997 and 1998 Currently, in addition to 18 Regional Centers, 145 study centres are also in operation in the year 1998. In the next phase the University may cover all other locations, hitherto not covered.

On an average IGNOU and other agencies are using teleconferencing 10-20 days in a month for various programmes (5 hours in a day with 60/90 minutes slots). The University has used approximately 495 hours in 1997 and the School of Management has used extensively (190 hours), followed by Social Sciences, Continuing Education and Humanities. Other agencies such as government, non-government and private organisations have used TC apart from IGNOU (approximately 700 hours since 1995). The recent major expansion made by the School of Management to divert 40% of its regular counselling sessions to tele-counselling in the year 1998 may lead other Schools also to resort to tele-counselling in the academic years 1999 and 2000 onwards.

India has a strong network of distance/open education system wherein 8 provincial open universities and a National Open University are in operation. Many more are in the pipeline and according to the National Policy of Education each Provincial government is expected to establish an Open University. In this direction, IGNOU has already established Distance Education Council to coordinate all provincial open Universities and correspondence institutes. Currently, all other universities`)has established their own network of Regional Centres, study centres, work centres, etc. which would be fulfilling their requirements. Similarly, a few CCIs too have established their own network of centres, especially in their operational areas. Thus all Open Universities have established approximately more than 1000 study centres. Many more study centres in different forms may come up in future.

An OPENET a network of Open Universities has already been created by the IGNOU (DEC), in the Ninth Five Year Plan. This is essentially a network of physical intellectual and academic resources of all OUs in India, developed and managed in such a way that becomes the knowledge resource for all aspiring learners in the country. In this direction the DEC using the OPENET should identify priority areas to take distance education, especially professional vocational and technical education to disadvantaged sections.

A few such projects /programmes have already been implemented by the University viz. Panchayati Raj programme for 58,000 elected members of panchayats in four selected districts of Madhya Pradesh and Tannery Workers Training programme (in collaboration with the ministry of Rural Areas and Employment and

Technology Mission GOI) in the years 1996 and 1997. The Tannery workers vocational qualification project has been implemented in 6 districts of Tamil Nadu province enrolling 200 students in the first batch. The GOI (MHRD) has given another project to IGNOU (Women's Education Unit (WEU), to empower disadvantaged women through distance education in the country. The Women's Education Unit of IGNOU has proposed a few six-month certificate courses for the disadvantaged women in the areas of viz. "Legal literacy and empowerment ". These courses would be designed for the development of skills aimed at enhancing women's productive ability. Areas such as education and training, organisation, leadership, management and computer literacy, confidence building and elements of conscientisation would be emphasized.

The Women's Education Unit (WEU) has proposed collaborations and partnerships with agencies like Government and Non-Government (NGOs) organisations in need assessment and final delivery of courses to disadvantaged groups using new technologies and networks. The WEU is planning to establish 150 teleconferencing receiving-end nodes over a five-year period in selected provinces where the disadvantaged population including SC/ST is about 45%. The Unit has proposed to make use of the DPEP network and IGNOU's network which are available in these states.

Yashwantrao Chavan Maharashtra Open University

The approach followed at YCMOU is quite scientific in the sense that total quality management was planned for as a significant concern right from the beginning.

Accordingly, YCMOU made arrangements to:

- develop a quality system for the university;
- develop a total quality management model for the university;
- implement the quality system in the university; and
- develop and establish a mechanism to perpetuate total quality management in the university.

The quality system in conceptual terms has already been articulated in a preliminary quality manual, indicating clearly the dimensions of quality that will be attended to (namely the *time* a function will be executed, the *product* or *service* specified, and the *costs* involved) as well as the administrative and operational mechanisms needed to materialise the system. The work done so far includes a policy decision to:

- appoint management representatives to co-ordinate the overall quality assurance activities;
- set up a quality advisory council consisting of officers and experts who will be responsible for implementing this quality assurance programme;
- establish a quality assurance centre for total quality management—such a centre would be entrusted with the responsibility of supervision and verification of the quality standards laid down; and
- organise training programmes for in-house staff to implement the quality system.

Further additional work has been completed:

- detailed documents on the interface of departments; the responsibilities of every division, centre, and section of the university; and procedures for reviewing the feedback received from various units, as well as those for revising the details and distribution of the reports; and

— procedures for documentation, both at the institutional and the departmental levels, including those required to materialise the quality system. Accordingly, departmental processes have already been analysed and component activities have been identified.

ICTs-enhanced Education at Naptional Open School

In India, despite impressive achievement in schooling, about 40 million children are out of school; most of them are school dropouts and possess stable literacy. It is in the interest of the economic & social development of the country that the school dropouts & neo-literate are provided with an effective target focussed alternative channel of learning. Since such people can not go to school, alternative modalities must deliver education at their doorstep. In such educational scenario of the country, the only viable mechanism of delivering good quality school education to such people is through open schooling and distance education mode.

The Government of India in 1989 established the National Open School as an autonomous organisation under the Department of Education, Ministry of Human Resource Development. The National Open School (NOS) provides an alternative channel to thousands of drop-outs, unemployed or working adults, women, disabled, socially and economically backward classes, socially disadvantaged groups or those learner who wish to update their educational attainments but are unable to be full time learners. NOS offer both academic and vocational courses at Foundation, Secondary and Senior Secondary levels. Besides, NOS also offers basic education and community development programmes.

NOS is also venturing into open elementary education programmes from this year. The National Open School operates through strong network of 10 Regional Centres and 886 Accredited Institutions (Study Centres) spread all over the country.

The enrolment in NOS is growing every year since its inception in 1989. The percentage growth of enrolment is phenomenal. It is as high as 70%. The Graph-1 shows the percentage enrolment growth of enrolment in NOS. Presently, the cumulative strength of NOS in various courses is about 626 thousand candidates. The cumulative enrolment indicates the total number of students taken admission in NOS since its inception.

The large volume of enrolment itself is suggestive of using information technology for its success. Secondly, the time bound delivery and accuracy are the crux of the open schooling system, which can be achieved only by means of computerization. Thirdly, provision of efficient and effective student support services needs a higher degree of automation. Fourthly, providing required and accurate information to the students in the quickest possible time can be achieved only by means of using computers. Last but not the least, one can not remain untouched with the technological advancement all around and think of progress.

With the advent of Internet and web technologies, the whole educational scenario, particularly the open schooling and distance education, is changing. It is greatly felt that only by means of information and communication technology, it is possible to reach the masses. In order to provide better, fast, accurate and efficient services and support to the students in terms of academic as well as administrative, all major areas of application were undertaken for computerization. Before we discuss the application areas in detail, let us take a view of the infrastructure and the set up available in NOS.

The Computer Centre of NOS has come a long way since it made a small beginning with only two personal computers in 1989. The Computer Centre is now equipped with latest hardware and software. There is Local Area Network (LAN) with centralise database system having a powerful Pentium-II based file server and fifteen nodes called intelligent terminals. The Local Area Network is based on star topology using 16 port hub and UTP connections. The individual units/ sections/departments have also been hooked up in the network. In addition to main Computer Centre, desk computers of Pentium series and HP Desk Jet printer were provided to senior officers and other functionaries for their smooth functioning and promoting greater efficiency. To make the information more on-line, these individual officers have also been hooked up in the network.

A separate DTP unit with Seven Pentium-II machines and four Laser jet printers have been set up to look after the voluminous work of printing and production. In order to cope up with large volume of printing of student data, two high-speed line printers are installed.

In addition to the above set-up at the head office in Delhi, the regional centres are also provided with one/

two computers and printer to facilitate the services further to the students. Besides, Pentium-II based Laptop computers have been provided to the Chairman and three Heads of the Departments making their mobility more effective and efficient. Looking to the induction of Internet technology, NOS is provided with six different Internet connections enabling its staff members to have access to Internet.

The basic Operating System installed is Advance Novell Network 4.0 as the main operating system for LAN and windows-95 at the user end. Besides, the following system software are used; RDBMS, Visual FoxPro, MS-Office, Page-Maker. Indica & Akshar for windows are used as Hindi Fonts. In addition the Application Development Team develops all the User Application Software in house. The following areas of applications have been computerised in NOS

As part of the computerization, the admission form of NOS was redesigned as per need of computer and efforts were made to codify most of the items of the admission form. In this direction we developed a 9-didgit registration number for each student. In the on-line system of Student Information System, giving enrolment number of any student brings the complete and updated status of that student. This helped greatly in dealing the query from any student.

Data Entry of admission forms is done study centre wise with a number of in-built checks provided in the software package. The in-built checks are valid student's enrolment number, valid subject codes, valid date of birth, valid course level course etc. After data entry and its verification, study centres wise Database file as well as the cumulative student database as the central database is generated. After Finalisation of student data, study centre wise checklist, Identity card and confirmation letter for each student is printed and dispatched to each study centre. For the year 1997, the admission forms of 112 thousands students data were processed.

Printing of study materials distribution report for each study centre indicating the medium-wise/ subject-wise number of candidates. This enabled the mailing branch to dispatch the study materials to the study centre for each student. Earlier the study materials were used to be dispatched on expected number of students, which used to create number of problems. With the help of this dispatch report, the distribution of study materials got smoothened and error-free. In addition various statistical reports such as Course wise, Medium wise, Sex wise, Region/state wise, Subject wise, Age wise, Category wise, etc are printed and provided to the management as MIS reports. During the processing, we also capture the background information of each student such as parent's education, family income, rural or urban etc. Based on these information reports are provided which help in taking decisions for policy making.

Prior to computerization, each student from each study centre used to fill up an examination form and they used to mention even those subjects whom they had cleared in earlier examinations or such subjects, which have not been taken in their admission.

In NOS, there is a system of credit accumulation where the awards achieved by a student are maintained in a student result database as his credit. This database is updated with every examination result till the candidate gets a certificate. In total, the student gets nine chances to get a certificate during the five years of registration period. Due to credit accumulation system the processing of result is more cumbersome as the awards achieved by the students in earlier examination are also taken into consideration. The student gets a combined result showing his current and old awards together. This was possible only by means of computer, as such exercise was not possible manually. For every examination, we developed a concept of current student result master and cumulative student result master.

Processing the current awards file and merging it with the old master result database generates the current result master. The following activities are involved in the result processing.

— Punching of awards at two different places from the computerised award lists as well as manual awards. This is done to ensure the 100% accuracy in the result processing.

— As a result of the above process two databases are prepared of the awards. These two databases are then collated and the discrepancy is eliminated, if any.

— Posting of current awards for each subject to each student record prepared as the examination database.

— Processing of result as per the passing and other examination criteria of NOS already laid down in the scheme of examination and conversion of fictitious roll number with the original roll number. The credit transfer cases from CBSE are also taken into consideration while processing the result.

— Merging of the above-prepared current result database with the old student master which contains the old achievement of each such student.

- Creation of the final student result database from where the following documents are printed :
  - Student result gazette
  - Mark statement for each student on pre-printed stationery
  - Migration certificate for all certified candidate
  - School certificate for all certified candidate
- Dispatch of these documents to study centre for further information and distribution to each student.
- Processing of Result Withheld cases for Unfair Means committee. The decision of this committee is taken into consideration and the result of such candidates and processed as per the procedure discussed above. In similar manner the result processing of Result later cases are dealt with.

As the number of enrolment and programmes has been increasing, so was the requirement of more number of books. The growth in number of books produced is remarkable and is directly proportional to the growth of enrolment. During, the year 1998-99 6.5 million books were printed. For printing of this huge volume of books, 1200 MTs of printing and 150 MTs of pulp paper were required. We developed a Publication Management package NOS-PUB. Right from calculation of paper requirement to the processing of printer's bill all the activities fall under this system. The following activities are done under the in-house developed Publication Management Package. *Assessment is done for the total number of candidates to be admitted taking into account the trends of last three years admission.

— Assessment of subject-wise/medium wise total number of student.

— Calculation of paper requirement for the printing of study materials after taking the balance stock into consideration.

— Creation and maintenance of database of Empanelled printing presses.

— Random allocations of printing jobs to the empanelled printing presses.

— Processing of Printer's bills.

The store is completely computerised through in-house developed Inventory Management System. The inputs in the system are only purchase voucher and item issue indents. On the basis of these inputs the inventory master file and inventory transaction files are updated on-line. The system takes care of daily Receipts, daily issue, balance stock as on date, re-order Level, Stock register, Consumption reports & requirement reports. Besides, various other daily, monthly and annual reports are taken.

The Accounts and Audit of NOS is fully computerised. For basic accounting the readymade package TCS-EX of Financial Accounting is used. With the help of this package the annual budget is taken out well in time. The package provides on line updating of all accounting files. This helped in bringing trial balance and Income and Expenditure statement at any point of time in the financial year. Besides, a package NOS-FIN is developed in-house which takes care of salary Slips, annual GPF Account, Income-tax statement and various other accounting work.

The Library is computerised with UNESCO information storage and retrieval package CDS-ISIS. There are about 10,000 books and other items in the library. There are about 100 CD-titles on different subjects available in the library. It is also connected with Delhi Library Network and has an Internet connection. The Internet connection at library has eased the academics in getting information on any field or topic within no time. One multi-media workstation is installed in the library. The availability of any book or item becomes very easier with the help of computer and also the location and status of any book or item. With the help of the in-house developed package NOSLIB the issue & return of any book or item is located.

NOS has a large production of instructional study materials. About 600 titles are prepared for printing as study materials for the students. Data entry of all academic and vocational study materials are done in-house using MS-Word and later page making & typefaces are done for preparation of CRC. Besides, the quarterly magazines, leaflets and other publications are prepared in-house. It has been taken up as a very important project where a databank would be created for item after its due evaluation. Such item bank would be used for setting of question paper. Random set of papers would be done without repetition of the same item in different sets of paper. The whole project is computerised and at present we are in the process of creation of item databank.

Keeping in view the growth of information technology and the prominent position that education has occupied on the Internet, the National Open School is also in the process of developing a web based environment in order to enable students to have access to high quality education. NOS have its web site at www.nos.org helping to disseminate information about itself. Clicking this site address will bring the user to the NOS Home Page indicating its address and telephone numbers and provides different menu buttons with hyperlinks to reach the different information pages of NOS. We have also planned to put the results on the Internet for its access to the students. With the development of its own web site, NOS would soon be offering courses on-line through Internet, the first one being a one year Certificate in Computer Applications (CCA). By harnessing the power of one of the most impactful technology, NOS also hopes to offer all its courses and programmes on-line in the near future.

Another ambitious project is the development of an electronic network of Internet based school known as Indian Open Schooling Network (IOSN). IOSN will bring together a large number of Internet based schools all over India and will have great potential to enhance the teaching and learning process by providing a common communication platform. IOSN will also have linkages with the Commonwealth Electronic Network for School and Education (CENSE), thereby expanding its scope to become a national grid which in turn will be linked to its international counterparts. At present about 30 schools have been connected under IOSN.

As part of the computerization, all the staff members were given training in computer for enhancing their work efficiency. Few staff members were given specific training in DTP work and few in Database management system as per their requirement. As part of in-service training, the staff of computer centre were given training in Internet, HTML and JAVA.

7

Distance Education: Emerging Trends

Distance education has developed so to speak unnoticeably—as industrialized education during the last 120 years, and if, over and above, it is maintained that this model of education will be of great importance for tackling important educational tasks at present and in the future, then it is necessary to comment on the reservations voiced by those critics of culture as they would otherwise underline that such a concept will be questionable, if not dangerous. Distance education provides necessary technical and organizational preconditions for a universal admission to continued and higher education.

An analysis of statistics about distance education reveals that millions of distant students do indeed profit from this industrialized way of education. Often enough it offers them the only way towards the desired education as all other ways are barred by lack of funds or by other circumstances. Comparison with the conditions under which face-to-face-instruction takes place in the schools of the Federal Republic of Germany as well as in those of other countries can be used to show that we are dealing with school systems organized according to class structures in which access to secondary schools and universities remains restricted, so that people continue to suffer from the inequality of educational opportunities.

The distance education system is mainly dependent on indirect interaction and communication it has, so to speak, completed its seculization. The interaction between teacher and student is objectified by rational teaching techniques and the use of technical media to such a degree that even relicts of archaic attitudes are no longer possible. In instructional face-to-face situations, however, one can still find them.

The traditional teaching and learning behaviours are obviously so stable that they resist the use of technical media and the application of principles of industrialization. The communicative structure of traditional instruction in the classroom depends on limited number of students. Probably 120 students would be the largest possible number in a lecture hall.

A radical new approach was needed to overcome this limitation and to make possible the instruction of large and extremely large groups of students which appeared when the general level of education had to be raised as a consequence of industrialization.

Distance education is such an approach. The archaic forms of imparting knowledge and skills could be characterized with regard to their media structure by the negative statement that they functioned without any technical medium. This means that the teachers relied on the medium of the words spoken directly to the student. Whether the teacher was a medicine man, a prophet, a shaman or a priest, he or she always communicated knowledge orally. The oral teaching of those priest-teachers must, however, not be understood in a modern sense, as the words were not yet isolated from their original context. Today, distance education developed considerably further by becoming largely independent from the traditional ties. This opens up new perspectives which have not yet been noticed and new problems which have not yet been tackled by experts of the methodology of teaching and learning.

Distance education can be egalitarian, as the application of technical media overcomes some of the traditional barriers to educational opportunity. These media enable schools and universities to extend their instructional systems in such a way that every capable citizen can profit from learning if they wish - even after their school or college years.

In the present historical -economic situation of highly industrialized societies the increased availability and accessibility of education thus assumes a special importance, as the further democratizing of society will increase the educational needs of all citizens considerably. More and more of them will lay claim to their human right of education. It is safe to say that such an increased demand of education can only be satisfied with the help of industrialized forms of education.

Distance education provides for instruction in which teaching and learning have been secularized to a high degree, as the relation between teacher and students has been isolated from its traditional social context and objectified. Teacher and students do not interact as persons in their totality, but as special teaching and learning functions which operate only in order to reach the defined goals. The numinous, however, needs the social context in order to be able to express itself.

Distance education enables and facilitates instruction without repressive actions in the sense that arbitrary acts of teachers - as well as of students - are cut out as technical mediation and the required division of labour have objectified instruction. If there are institutional or direct dependencies, as, for instance, in the military services and in vocational training, they will be less effective for the same reasons.

Distance education is principally mediated instruction. It cannot take place without the help of technical media. Without the mechanization of the presentation of the contents of instruction and of the feedback activities it would not be possible to start, optimize and control it. Distance education has cut the three bonds which ties face-to-face instruction to special places, special times and special persons. It is normally characterised by affective neutrality—as here the teaching and learning is not achieved by an interaction of persons, but, strictly speaking, of isolated functions. This does not necessarily mean that technically mediated instruction cannot be affective at all. Now and then one can find initial stages of it. However, it remains safe to say that in distance education the social relations tend to be neutral.

Traditional instruction in the classroom is oriented to a particular frame of reference: a given teacher teaches a given learning group in a given temporal and locational situation. Industrialised instruction, on the other hand, disregards particular conditions of this kind, as it has a more general, if not principally universal frame of reference.

Distance education tends, indeed, towards universal application. It uses a language which is taken out of its originally associated surroundings, and is thus free of its context. The technically mediated communication of necessity remains unaffected by particular circumstance, as it addresses students everywhere. In the classroom the communicative acting is determined by reciprocal expectations of behaviour. This means that the teacher who acts expects the students to react in a special way and vice versa.

The expected reactions take place with a higher degree of probability the more the interacting persons have internalized a role consensus and the more the expected behaviour has become ritualized by habit. In industrialised distance education the segments of interaction are constructed on the basis of conditioned prognoses and conditioned imperatives.

Particular sequences of a global behaviour become objectified and isolated. In face-to-face instruction the dominant mechanism of acquisition is the internalisation of roles. The students live up to expectations by internalising the norms of the group. Knowledge and skills are transported by means of this particular role identification, role taking and role performance.

In distance education, however, the teaching-learning process is reduced to the learning of skills and qualifications. Every measure in this system has the sole function of achieving this goal. Communicative action and role performance are cut out. In face-to-face instruction the social interaction helps to maintain the institution. Teachers and students are subject to external and internal control. In distance education, however, the indirect interaction is subject to the attainment of the learning goals by using means to an end.

Significance of Interactive Distance Learning

Interactive Distance learning (IDL) refers to a portfolio of application and networking solutions that can be (and are being) implemented by universities, K-12 schools, corporations, and government agencies to enable them to enhance the education and research process. IDL solutions establish telecommunication links between education receivers and various sources of knowledge over geographic areas that may span a metropolitan segment, a whole state, or the entire country.

These sources of knowledge are not limited to distance learning providers, such as universities and corporate training centres; they also encompass information and processing resources, such as libraries, supercomputer centres, and museums. The required links may involve voice communications, video communications, data communications, or a combination of these media.

The quality of the distance learning programmes is a function of the selected type of solution and the particular needs of the distance learners.IDL solutions can address many of the challenges facing education and training institutions.

Educators and administrators who appreciate the positive value of telecommunications are investing school capital and operating funds in IDL technology; in many schools and colleges, telecommunications has become a line item in the operating budget. New technologies, namely satellite communication, fibre optic cable and computers have dramatically enhanced educational capabilities.

By providing communication links, telecommunications can overcome distance barriers that hamper development. Thus through the use of new communication technologies, access to good educational programmes can be greatly extended to large audiences in rural and remote areas with tremendous flexibility in subject matter content and in locations served. Corollary to these technological expansions, the area of education which is considered to be fastest growing today is that of distance education.

Distance education, based on the use of modern communications and multimedia materials, has proved to be the major new movement in human resource development in the current decade. The ability to cope with rapid changes in the higher education system will become the primary measure of success, of both micro and macro levels, as we approach the 21st century. Many societies have shifted from industrial era to information era, and others are fast moving in that direction. The volume of information that becomes available, doubles every four to five years. Teachers have to become experts in helping learners navigate through this sea of information rather than pretending to be effective transformers of that information into knowledge.

Students must be trained to bring about that information. Those who survive this information explosion will be able to deal with it effectively and even more importantly, acquire knowledge. Education is going to be number one amongst the great world industries, within which will flourish an educational machine technology that will provide tools such as the individually selected and articulated two-way TV and an inter-continentally networked documentary call up system operative on any home two-way set.

Emergence of ICTS has generated a potential of a sea-change in the education system all over the world. Print, radio, television, audio-video cassettes, tape-recorders, overhead/slide projectors, filmstrips, etc., which permit only one-way communication have become old educational technologies and have lost novelty in the developed world.

The last one decade has seen emergence of a series of new, electronic-based innovations in the field of higher education, which permit vision, sound, data with inter-activity. Information highways are high speed data networks used to transport information and link people who want to be connected with others.

Teletext and Video-text are the two new information age services that will soon be widespread among home and business users. Teletext is a one-way service in which pages of information from a central database are broadcast on a regular television signal.

Video-text is a more sophisticated two-way service using telephone lines. E-mail, tele-conferencing (audio and video) and computer conferencing are common activities on the internet and other electronic networks. The words information highway reflect speed, volume, powers, and efficiency.

With the information highways becoming a reality in many countries, Conferencing Technologies (CT) have come to be used in a large way in collaborative distance and open learning. The success of CTs will depend on the extent to which learning tasks, such as attentiveness, idea generation, concept elaboration, feedback, etc., are fulfilled. The CTs reduce the teachers' teaching functions without reducing the academic rigour. Since generally the adults are the participants of CTs, a collaborative type of learning is necessary. When integrated into the whole learning context, CTs offer sufficient flexibility to the learners and the educators. Thus, a virtual classroom can be created in which the class is taught using the satellite, microwave or cable linkages between them.

There is no doubt that an extensive emergence of electronic-based technology in the field of education is in the offing. However, one must not forget limitations in its use, especially in the developing countries.

The advocates of the modern technologies in education presuppose that the learners have access to a wide range of high specification information and communication technologies; that these technologies can be used at time and in circumstances that are convenient for learners and optimal for effective study; and the learners have sufficient familiarity or experience of using them.

Unfortunately all these presumptions are far from true so far as learners in developing countries are concerned. Though there may be television in the house, there is certainly a claim of all members of the family for using TV for entertainment purposes. Not many students have access to VCRs because of the costs. Even those who have VCRs may not always be able to use them in view of the competing demand for TV time by others. PC and modems are absent in most of the learner houses in the developing countries.

Multiplicity of languages used in the same country, as in India, also poses severe problems in reaching distance education to different parts through the broadcasting/networking systems. Thus, there are severe limitations in the use of high specification informa-tion and communication technology in the developing countries. It may take two to three decades to reduce these limitations to an insignificant level.It will be difficult to protect national, state or provincial boundaries from distance education. Governments will have to deal with the question, sooner or later, whether they would like to be net exporters or net importers of education. The answer of course is quality.

The distance teaching institutions, in particular, will have to demonstrate superior quality of education that will override the public's preconceptions of the status of better- known, more conventional institutions as they enter into the distance teaching world via the internet. There is also the question of access.

The high specification information and communication technology can be accessed only by the rich and the very rich in the developing countries who can afford to have a number of TVs, modems, computers and can afford to pay for long distance call charges, etc. separately for entertainment and education purposes. The proportion of such learners is microscopically small. Since they belong to the elitist society they would, anyway, have been well educated in the conventional system of education.

Electronic-based technologies will dominate the education scenario in the developed countries. The 21st century will give rise to electronic educational institutions which will provide information on education and training needs and opportunities; quality control; accreditation; coherent curricula and other concomitant services. Many of the instructors or tutors may not belong to the educational institutions but will be independent contractors. Nor would it be necessary for learners to be registered with an educational institution. The educational institutions may only collect and deliver payments for fees and royalties to the owners of the software or the telecom companies.

Unless the less developed countries are able to create an appropriate technological infrastructure to support the kind of learning needed in the 21st century, they would be left far behind. Building up of information highways are the *sine quo non* of the modern system. The need of the 21st century will be to exploit the information highway to the fullest possible extent. In order to make education accessible to all and to make it meaningful, exciting and interesting, a new technology need to be linked with the process of learning.

The new technology is not only capable of overcoming the barriers that distance presents, but also changes the very nature of the instructional process. It is technology that made the move from correspondence to distance education possible.

If the demands of the society for education are to be met successfully, we will have to switch over to an alternative approach of unconventional mode of distance education through mass communication technology currently available. Modern communication technologies have the potential to bypass several stages and sequences in the process of development encountered in earlier decades.

In order to avoid structural dualism, modern education technology must reach out to the most distant areas and to the most deprived sections of beneficiaries simultaneously with the areas of comparative affluence and ready availability.

Asynchronous communications for Distance Education

Use of asynchronous communications for education and training has been popularized into the rapidly growing metaphor of Asynchronous Learning Networks (ALN), many of us have become more than a little upset at some of the misconceptions and misapplications beginning to occur with respect to applying computer networking to higher education. Historically it is no comfort that this is the process that often occurs when new ideas based upon visions become popularized and introduced with a limited understanding of the their roots. Furthermore the administrative practices, management, and policies currently associated with distance education are encouraging exactly the wrong approach to utilize the technology to improve learning and increase the quality of the educational delivery process.

It is quite clear historically in the field of Management Information Systems that new information and computer system technologies can be misdirected if the underlying human organizations and customs are not adapted to make the best use of the technology. In US, college tuition can range from approximately $3,000 to $30,000 for an academic year. Recently the concept of the average student being right out of high school has been overturned and the majority of college students have been, or are, in the work place. Many distance students being attracted to the ALN programs are the more valuable employees who never considered that they could take the time needed for regular courses. At the graduate level students in technical fields seek companies for jobs that will pay for their courses on a part time basis.

Clearly many of the current ALN programs have been designed to "skim the cream" of the crop that these students represent. Higher education in the U.S. does not have a very effective lobby and many state supported institutions are facing, at best, semi-static budgets that are in effect cuts that cause increased tuition. The true costs at most state institutions would result in a tuition $15,000 or more if the student had to pay full costs. Outstanding private institutions cost about $25,000 but are subsidized, in addition, by endowments. Today, one could start a pure electronic virtual university for about 2000 students with a tuition of around $15,000, where every single faculty member was paid a flat $150,000 a year and class size would be in the 25-30 student range. The initial funding to get off the ground would be fifteen million dollars. This would also allow each accepted student to take some initial courses free of charge. This cost is less than a new building on most college campus in the United States. Clearly there are no colleges where all faculty get that salary but if it did, it would certainly attract a faculty of top educators.

Today most institutions would rather spend that chunk of funds on a new building. At many institutions distance education is a separate administrative operation from the academic departments. Furthermore, the administration of distance education and the responsibility for the delivery of the courses is often in the hands of the distance education administration and not under the faculty in the department that normally has the academic governance authority over the face-to-face courses and their content.

A significant percentage of the courses in distance education, at a growing number of institutions, are taught by adjuncts and non faculty staff. Since the cost of such courses is usually lower, the administration comes to view such programs as a sources of a "profit" in the cash flow. The distance learning operation often works on a fixed fee and the remainder of the tuition paid by the student is returned to the general budget funds.

Challenges of Commercialization

Current trends seem to indicate that there is going to be a tremendous long term shakeout of marginal institutions that cannot deliver quality education or meaningful full degree programs. We are entering a period of what may be intense competition and commercialism for higher education that will spread beyond national boundaries. The commercial training programs to aid students to prepare for the GREs, GMATs, and MCATs are indications of the future There are a number of commercial companies that advertise that they will create a virtual university/college on the web for any institution. They will come to your college and in five days train the professors how to transfer their courses to the web, how to teach on the web, and they will manage the whole operation for you. It does not matter to them what subject you are talking about, they have a single approach that is suppose to work for any discipline and any degree program. There is no awareness that the best way to teach by using the technology may be completely different than what is normally done in the physical face-to-face environment. There is no recognition of the need to rethink the education process and the associated methodologies.

The growing number of these academic consultants and web based real-estate developers for the virtual campuses are evidence of the commercialization process that seems to be overtaking higher education. Many companies are backing off from their sizable investment in internal training programs are turning back to colleges and universities to take up the slack. They find the idea of distance education attractive to reach their nationally and internationally spread workforce. However, they speak in terms of such concepts as "just in time training" like learning is analogous to an inventory system. They confuse learning and training and are pushing institutions to offer small chunks of education such as certificate programs that are also degree accredited.

While there is a role for colleges and universities to deliver training, the traditional objective of higher education is to deliver a product to the "student" that is the "mastery" of the subject and allows him or her to advance their career even if that means giving the student the ability to get qualify for a new job in a different organization.

Concepts of "just in time training" and training in current technologies, in limited packages, is an educational mission that serves the company and not the student. With industry picking up an increasing share of the costs of tuition for students they are beginning to influence the objectives of the educational mission and it may not always be in a direction beneficial to the interests of the student. This may be a more long term force of commercialization than the prior one but it is probably a more dangerous one. While there are movements to try to do away with tenure in the educational system in the U.S., it is not the more obvious lobby efforts that are worrisome. What is of concern is the subtle administrative practices that can, over a long period of time, significantly reduce tenure as an important component of higher education and eliminate the safeguard it represents for the educational process. The more insidious approach is the hiring of full time "qualified" staff to do teaching and the necessary use of adjuncts.

Young untenured faculty are hired in great number and they are encouraged to focus on research and seeking funds for research. They are alleviated from teaching many undergraduate courses and these are taken over by full time staff, regular adjuncts, and even "visiting" professors. While the untenured faculty think this is fine, it is fundamental change in higher education objectives by decreasing the importance of faculty performance in education at the undergraduate level. What is not realized is that some of these untenured faculty are being groomed for those staff positions when it becomes clear they will not succeed to get tenure. What they are judged on is their ability to bring in research funding and generate publications. Of course the long term implication of this is that the tenure decision is no longer viewed as important or serious. If they don't succeed they can become staff. They will end up as contract research appointments or full time teaching staff.

The condition to get tenure will become so stiff that only a negligible number will get through that filter. A few decades of this and the tenured faculty will be a true minority of those teaching and gradually fade away. Today, a degree program in some technical fields formulated around advertised jargon in the marketplace rather than meaningful bodies of scientific and technical knowledge. It is like a degree in sociology would become a degree in the behavior of the X-generation because advertisement firms wish to hire people who can graduate and be prepared to immediately design adds for that market group.

Industry is sometimes more interested in the student being certified in a particular software system then in obtaining an understanding of the fundamentals and theoretical principles that underlie all such systems. Over the past few decades many institutions in the U.S. have gone from situations where the majority of the salaries at the institution were faculty salaries to a situation today where a majority of the salaries are in administration and non tenure lines for research and teaching staff, sometimes referred to as research faculty, adjunct faculty, and/or fellows.

The technology is moving quickly to the point where a book is going to become software (including programs, video, and sound material) and that is going to lead to much conflict since all these nice distinctions completely break down. The Collaborative Hypertext concept would lead to dynamic knowledge bases developed collaboratively by the students and the instructor and updated with each new offering of the course. It would completely replace, in the long run, the text book and each new course offering would provide a CD-ROM of the current state of the knowledge base.

The sizable difference between adjunct pay and faculty pay is exactly what leads to associated labor - management problems and some mistrust of administrative intentions on the part of the faculty. It is an unhealthy long term motivation factor. All this might sound like a great economic opportunity to administrators. The use of adjuncts is actually an important slack resource that needs to be employed to allow for swings in load requirements that can occur because of short term research commitments. Furthermore there is justification for some number of full time teaching staff to handle the training missions of the universities. However, adjuncts and teaching staff should be under the direct supervision of the faculty in charge of a course and they should be reviewed by the appropriate faculty committees to be qualified for the courses they teach. In many situations such as separate distance learning programs this is not the case.

We are entering a world where students need the flexibility of determining when they are remote and when they are not. A clear distinction will be hard to maintain and gradually become meaningless. There are many aspects where the distance learning program has significant impact on the regular program. For example, the presence of videos of class lectures in the library has been a significant aid to the regular student who has missed one or more lectures because of sickness or work commitments. It has also proved useful for those with language problems who need to listen more than once to a lecture.

However, there is no library mission or budget to provide the tapes of courses for access by regular students. As a result the tape collection availability is a far more limited in hours than the normal hours for the library. The tape library comes out of the distance learning office budget and not out of the library. When we talk about software to support this area we talk about communication protocols and human roles built into the software to aid the instructor in promoting equal participation and facilitate the communication process. We see an instructor as having a mental model of complex problem solving in that domain and trying to convey to the students the structure of that model and how to adapt their thinking process to learn and integrate that model. Whether it be engineering design, computer programming, literary analysis, historical understandings of events, or whatever, it is still that fundamental endeavor.

Future of Net-oriented Distance Learning

The Internet is the world's largest, most powerful computer network connecting personal computers, sophisticated mainframes, and high speed supercomputers around the globe. The arrival of the World Wide Web signals the beginning of some fundamental changes in how teaching, training, and self-directed learning will occur at all ages and stages of life. The World Wide Web as a vehicle for disseminating course materials and for creating active learning experiences within a classroom-based course.

Educators at all levels, from Kindergarten to adult training, are drawing a distinction between two fundamentally different approaches to teaching. In one, the goal is to transfer, as effectively and efficiently as possible, a concise and coherent block of information from the teacher or computer into the minds of the learners. Most existing computer-based training for adults has been designed with knowledge transfer in mind. Extraneous information is left out.

The emphasis is on individual learning and learners have a limited number of paths through the lesson. This approach works well for the training of basic skills in areas of knowledge that are well defined and stable. For most of us, though, the world just isn't that way. As adults we face one ill-defined problem after another. The specific facts that we have to know change so quickly that some knowledge becomes obsolete almost as soon as we master it. The knowledge-transfer approach doesn't prepare us well for a messy world in constant motion.

The World Wide Web, lends itself beautifully to constructivist, active learning. In 1989, a group of scientists at the European Laboratory for Particle Physics (CERN) in Geneva, Switzerland began developing an Internet tool that would link information produced by all of the CERN researchers. The tool provided a way to link textual information on different computers and created by different scientists. The object was to overcome issues of incompatibility and utilize a new way of linking made possible by computers, called "hypertext". Rather than presenting information in a linear or hierarchical fashion, hypertext permits information to be linked in a web-like structure. Nodes of information can be linked to other nodes of information in multiple ways. As a result, users can dynamically criss-cross the information web using pieces in the order most convenient to them.

The CERN project resulted in an innovative front-end to the Internet, now referred to as the World-Wide Web (WWW). The WWW provides users with a uniform and convenient means of accessing the vast resources of the Internet. In 1993, the National Center for Supercomputing Applications (NCSA) at the University of Illinois pushed the CERN scientists' idea further by creating a software tool called Mosaic. Mosaic is an easy to use graphical user interface that permits text, graphics, sound and video to be hyperlinked. Mosaic was the first of the Internet tools that are now referred to as " Web browsers". Other well-known browsers include Netscape and Microsoft's Internet Explorer. Web browsers permit users to connect to the Internet and facilitate accessing information located on another remote computer.

The Web browser links to the remote computer just long enough so that the information you need can be sent to your computer for you to view. Documents created to be viewed by a browser are formatted using Hypertext Markup Language (HTML). HTML solves incompatibility problems by using standardized tags which indicate such things as whether a piece of text should be plain, bold, italic, or linked to another piece of text. Pages of information on a computer formatted with HTML and accessible to someone with a Web browser, are referred to as "home pages" or "Web pages". The WWW and Web browsers have made the Internet a more user-friendly environment. The ability to integrate graphics, text, and sound into a single tool means that novice users do not have to struggle with such a steep learning curve. In addition, organizations and individuals can create home pages independently and link to other home pages on their own computers or to pages created by others on different computer systems.

The WWW can be used by the distance educator to build a classroom home page. The home page can cover information about the class including the syllabus, exercises, literature references, and instructor's biography. The instructor can also provide links to information on the WWW that would be useful to students in the class (e.g., research data on agricultural markets, global climate change, or space missions). Other links can access library catalogs or each student's individual home page. In addition, the home page can link students to a discussion list or listserv that set up for student communication. It is also a relatively simple matter to use the homepage to create forms that students can fill out and that will end up being sent to you as an e-mail message. A web server can be run on a personal computer or a UNIX workstation.

What makes the World Wide Web especially exciting is that it also allows you to create anchors that download files for you or allow you to send e-mail to an individual. The web thus makes it easy to gain access to data, software and people. It's a user-friendly front end to almost everything on the internet. Within a year or so, the mechanics of creating documents on the web will become transparent. Most publishers of word processing software are adding the capability of saving documents in web format to their ever-growing list of features. So far, however, the end result of using a word processor to create web pages directly may not be exactly what you had in mind. An active webwriter will want to know how to tweak the appearance of the documents and, for the moment, that requires some familiarity with HTML. HTML, or HyperText Markup Language, is easy to learn. To prepare a page for the web, you just embed special characters or tags in your document to tell your browser how to display a given word. For a computer trainer, learning the basics of HTML should take no longer than a weekend.

The Adobe Acrobat format is an alternative method for displaying content on the web. This allows complex page layouts to be used, but users of your materials must all have the proper helper application installed on their machines. In a corporate environment with software standards in place, this shouldn't be a problem. Once you have created your pages, you simply upload them to the server you'll be using. Most medium to large-sized corporations have already established a web presence, and many smaller companies have as well. Whether you purchase space on the machines of an internet provider or set up your own webserver, you need not be physically near the server itself.

Most maintenance can be done from a distance. Once the use of the web as a way to distribute course materials is second nature to you, the next phase is to take advantage of all the material that's out there beyond the walls of your institution. The more you incorporate such activities into your course, the more it will become transformed into an learner-centered environment and the less often you'll find yourself holding forth on center stage. If you can get friends and colleagues, both in and outside of your enterprise, to volunteer to answer questions, you've broadened the pool of experience available to your students. Newsgroups provide an invisible college of people helping people. They are a great source of up to the minute news about software releases, bugs, and workarounds. If you have your own newsserver, you can also set up internal newsgroups specific to your course to provide a space for students to exchange information on an ongoing basis. Most newsgroups maintain a list of frequently asked questions that have come up within that group. These can be a rich source of materials and pointers to other resources on the web. Most major software publishers have placed their technical notes on the web.

There are many sources of useful wares ready to be downloaded. FTPing and decompressing this software is handled transparently by your web browser. One can place an anchor on a page that refers to a file and all your users have to do is click on it to have it delivered to their desktop. Hundreds of home pages have already been developed for courses. Some of these home pages allow students to complete an entire course from the WWW and others are developed in conjunction with lectures delivered on-campus or by video or audio.

The net world is moving quickly towards greater interactivity and sensory engagement. There are several developments worth watching. Some websites allow you to click on a picture and hear a greeting or introduction in the form of a sound file. You have to wait for the file to download before hearing anything, though, which tries the patience of all but the most fervent websurfers.

For distance education, the usefulness of RealAudio is obvious. All of the spoken communication that makes up a bulk of a traditional class can be digitized and made available as needed. As long as this doesn't lead back to the "talk, chalk and a hairy arm" tradition, RealAudio could become a standard feature of distance education on the web.

Virtual Reality Modelling Language is an embryonic set of tools and conventions for portraying three-dimensional space on the web. Instead of seeing a static picture, you'll be able to hold your mouse down over a graphic and see it from multiple perspectives, zooming in for detail and veering in any direction. For distance education, this allows for a more intuitive depiction of content: imagine seeing bubbles labeled with all the major concepts in your course. Lines linking the bubbles represent the relationships among them. Zoom in on a bubble and you've arrived at a webpage describing it in more detail. You might also use VRML to create a simulated learning environment with a reference room, laboratory, and help desk.

Java is a language for writing small programs (applets) that are downloaded as part of a web page. This will allow the web to take on most of the characteristics of the interactive multimedia you would find on a CD-ROM.

MOO stands for Multi-user dimension, Object-Oriented, which doesn't at first convey much about its meaning. A MOO is a shared virtual space that people can help create from their own computers. You can set up your conference room the way you like it and invite others to join you there. At present, most MOOs are text-based. When they begin to become more graphical, (soon) they will become the most popular places to be in cyberspace. These developments, and others, will make distance education more and more practicable on the web as time goes on.

New technologies with new applications can significantly reduce the costs of school networking and significantly improve the networking capabilities available to students, teachers, and the general public. These economies will make it possible to provide universal access to educational networks, thereby advancing the causes of educational equity and school reform and ending the isolation of the traditional classroom. During the last few years, thousands of schools and hundreds of thousands of students and teachers have begun to develop the Internet into a major educational resource.

Within the community of educational researchers, the Internet is now an accepted standard. Network use is also growing rapidly throughout the larger educational community, but several factors have placed practical limits on this growth.

If a school cannot obtain adequate connectivity, its ability to overcome isolation will be limited. If it has no access to a server, its ability to publish materials online will be limited. If it has too few user devices for all students to participate in networking activities, the promise of equity will not be achieved. And if tools do not exist that enable students and teachers to use networks imaginatively and effectively to support their broader educational goals, the promise of educational reform will not be met. Overcoming each of these obstacles entails a technological challenge. In the following sections, we list these challenges and describe some mechanisms for meeting them.

For educational and community networks, cost and access are the primary concerns, and network architectures that neglect these factors are unlikely to be sustainable for very long. Shared infrastructure and broad applicability bring other educational benefits. They create network environments that are conducive to interdisciplinary and collaborative activities and to research projects that explore an ever-expanding scope of resources. We believe that these sorts of activities and projects can contribute effectively to educational reform. We find that the portions of networks with the highest development costs and the greatest need for cost reduction are precisely those with the fewest possibilities for shared infrastructure. To put the issue in colloquial terms, we must deal not so much with the problem of building the information superhighway as with building the information driveway that leads into the home or classroom.

Schools and communities should choose their network technologies and services strategically, with an eye toward how their choices will support and leverage the overall networking infrastructure. Broad infrastructure needs are a much more important consideration in developing educational and community networks than in planning private networks or networks that serve a limited number of public or nonprofit organisations. Even though educational programs have a specific focus, they inspire other activities, and they rely on other organisations for many kinds of resources.

Future Trends

With the development of the postal service in the 19 th century, commercial correspondence colleges provided distance education to students across the world. This trend continued well into the 20 th century with the advent of radio, television, and other media that allowed for learning at a distance. In the last decade, providing education at a distance has changed significantly as the use of computer-mediated learning, two-way interactive video, and other technologies has increased.

Many universities are making substantial investments in new technologies for teaching. In recent years, colleges and universities have spent a great deal of time and effort in looking inward to analyze the efficacy of learning through the use of technology. This includes policy papers, "how to" articles, and essays, as well as a limited, though not insignificant body of original research. With few exceptions, the bulk of these writings suggests that the learning outcomes of students using technology at a distance are similar to the learning outcomes of students who participate in conventional classroom instruction. The attitudes and satisfaction of students using distance learning also are characterized as generally positive.

The rapid evolution and advances in technology offer both the general public and faculty a dizzying array of challenges that are unprecedented. For the last four decades, the speed and storage capacity of computers have doubled every 18-24 months; the cost, size, and power consumption have become smaller at about the same rate. The bandwidth of computer networks has increased a thousandfold in just the last decade, and the traffic on the network continues to grow at 300-500 percent annually. For the foreseeable future, all of these trends will continue; the basic technology to support their continued advance exists now. Technology is having, and will continue to have, a profound impact on colleges and universities around the globe.

Distance learning, which was once a poor and often unwelcome stepchild within the academic community, is becoming increasingly more visible as a part of the higher education family. The higher education community has a lot to learn regarding how, and in what ways, technology can enhance the teaching/learning process, particularly at a distance. As with other educational innovations that have come before it, there is some danger that the innovations made possible through distance education are advancing more rapidly than our understanding of its practical uses. In the context of the research on distance learning and its effectiveness, more emphasis has been placed on the "utopian" possibilities of the technology and its potential to do as well as classroom-based instruction. But not enough "pragmatism" has been applied to allow for a discussion of distance learning's practical implications as a supplement to enhance teaching and learning.

There are at least three broad implications that can be derived from this review of the original research and the other literature. The first is that the notion of "access to college" in the distance learning context is unclear. Many of the advocates of distance learning tout access to college-level education as a *raison d'etre* for the proliferation of distance education. Indeed, in some states, public policy leaders are recommending using distance education in lieu of "bricks and mortar" learning.

Of particular concern is access as it relates to the efficacy of computer-mediated learning. Unlike two-way interactive video, where students and the instructor can see and talk to each other in a conventional classroom, computer-mediated learning requires special skills of students and more sophisticated technical support if students are to interact fully. The faculty role will change from being mainly a content expert ('the professor's job is to profess') to a combination of content expert, learning process design expert, and process implementation manager. Faculty also will be motivators and mentors, interpreters (especially of non-codified knowledge), and, as a colleague recently put it, 'expert learners'-people who lead the learning process by breaking the trail and setting the right personal example.

Technology can leverage faculty time, but it cannot replace most human contact without significant quality losses." Third, although the ostensible purpose of much of the research is to ascertain how technology affects student learning and student satisfaction, many of the results seem to indicate that technology is not nearly as important as other factors, such as learning tasks, learner characteristics, student motivation, and the instructor. The irony is that the bulk of the research on technology ends up addressing an activity that is fundamental to the academy, namely pedagogy-the art of teaching.

Bibliography

Bruwelheide, J. (1994). "Distance Education: Copyright Issues". In Willis, B. (ed.) *Distance Education Strategies and Tools*, Englewood Cliffs, NJ: Educational Technology Publications.

Carter, A. (1995). Developing Faculty Training for Interactive Distance Education. *Innovations in Education and Training International*, 32(2).

Ho, M. S. (1996). *learning and Teaching in Cyberspace: an empirical investigation of computer assisted instruction for geography.* Academic exercise. Dept. of Geography, Faculty of Arts and Social Sciences, National University of Singapore.

Kochmer, J., "Internet passport: Northwestnet's guide to our world online", Bellevue, *WA: NorthWestNet and Northwest Academic Computing Consortium*, Inc., 1995.

Moore, M.G., & Thompson, M.M., with Quigley, A.B., Clark, G.C., & Goff, G.G., "The effects of distance learning: A summary of the literature", *Research Monograph No. 2*, University Park, PA: The Pennsylvania State University, American Center for the Study of Distance Education (ED 330 321), 1990.

Portway, P., and Lane, C. (1992). *Technical Guide to Teleconferencing and Distance Learning*. San Ramon, CA: Applied Business telecommunications.

Reid, K. A. (1995). *Impact of Technology on learning effectiveness. AT&T CEDL Newsletter.*

Steeples, C., Goodyear, P. and Mellar, H. (1993). Flexible Learning in Higher Education: The use of Computer-Mediated Communications. *Computers and Education.*

Verduin, J.R., & Clark, T.A., *Distance education: The foundations of effective practice*, San Francisco, CA: Jossey-Bass Publishers, 1991.

Watkins, B., and S. Wright, 1991. *The Foundations of American Distance Education*, Dubuque, IA: Kendall/Hunt.

Williams, M., and Paprock, K. (1994). Instructional design in distance education. *The ED Journal*, 7(4).

Willis, B., *Distance education: A practical guide*, Englewood Cliffs, NJ: Educational Technology Publications, 1993.

Wurster, S. (1996). *Distance Education: Beneath the Surface.* Techtrends.

Index